RANDOM
SYMMETRIES

THE COLLECTED POEMS
OF TOM ANDREWS

RANDOM SYMMETRIES

THE COLLECTED POEMS OF TOM ANDREWS

Oberlin College Press

http://www.oberlin.edu/~ocpress

Some of the poems in this collection first appeared in *The Brother's Country* (Persea Books, 1990) and *The Hemophiliac's Motorcycle* (U. of Iowa Press, 1994).

Oberlin College Press would like to thank Mike Chitwood and Charles Wright for their help in assembling this edition.

Publication of this book was supported in part by a grant from the Ohio Arts Council.

Ohio Arts Council
A STATE AGENCY
THAT SUPPORTS PUBLIC
PROGRAMS IN THE ARTS

Library of Congress Cataloging-in-Publication Data

Andrews, Tom, 1961-2001.
    Random Symmetries: The Collected Poems of Tom Andrews / Tom Andrews.
        (The FIELD Poetry Series v. 13)
        I. Title.   II. Series.

LC: 2002094511
ISBN: 0-932440-92-4 (pbk.)

Contents

III

IV

25 Short Films About Poetry

The Temptation of Saint Augustine

Last Poems

TOM ANDREWS: AN APPRECIATION

Charles Wright

Here is what I said about Tom at his memorial service in New York City on November 16, 2001. Tom was singular and luminous, as is his work. All of us, each one of us, will leave a space, an emptiness, when we die. But all of us, when we go, will not, as Tom did, turn out a light.

Here is what I didn't say. Tom was probably the most naturally gifted writer to have ever gone through one of my writing classes. The leaves just burst from his fingers. He had that odd stance to the world and its language that made whatever he wrote seem new and just discovered, like treasure hauled up into the sealight from the ocean floor. He had an appointment, a destiny in him, that most of us lack, or are incapable of keeping. He was on his way to that appointment, punctual as ever, when he was cut down. Still, he left a fair amount of essential work, both poetry and prose. The poems are collected here: three complete volumes, with an interlude of prose poems. The last of the three, and the only unpublished complete volume—about St. Augustine—, gives a good idea of the direction the poet was headed: into the rarely visited, with one of those anonymous caravans that bring back unheard-of stories from the lands of the dead.

Tom rode motocross as a young man. "Fueled by Jesus" was one of the shirts he wore. Tom was in the *Guinness Book of World Records* at the age of 11—he clapped hands for over 14 consecutive hours. He was a hemophiliac. Not "brittle," but seriously enough to get himself seriously in trouble on many occasions. His classic little memoir, *Codeine Diary*, details some of this. And serious enough to have his fatal illness, a blood disorder, perhaps have some connection to one of the many transfusions he had to undergo.

I kept all of his poems from our workshops at the University of Virginia, two years worth. In going through them (from the mid-1980s) I was rather astounded to find that every one of them had found its way into his first book, *The Brother's Country*. Now, how many of us could claim such a sure sense of his path and the worth of his poems at such an early stage? Certainly no one I know. But Tom, as I say, had an appointment, just this side of Samarkand, it turned out, and was already on his way.

I'm not sure just how efficacious it is to talk about a body of work

that is just in the next room. Best to open the door and see for yourself. I
will say, however, that I think the St. Augustine poem, which culminates an
almost-lifelong absorption by Tom in the man's work and in his person
(Tom's own spiritual pulls and pushes are mirrored in Augustine's) is a
widening of the contemporary envelope. We all like to imagine that we
will pull off such a maneuver, and precious few are able to do so. Tom was,
and he did. Cold comfort, perhaps, to those of us who loved him, but
that's the course which literature lays out when it hangs your number on
your back. So, yes, some comfort indeed.

The Brother's Country

for my mother and father
for Jack and Julie Ridl
for Carrie

I

But in spite of my soul's leap out to him, at the end of its elastic, I saw him only darkly, because of the dark and then because of the terrain, in the folds of which he disappeared from time to time, to re-emerge further on. . .

—Samuel Beckett, *Molloy*

THE BROTHER'S COUNTRY

(John Andrews, 1956-1980)

1.

Beside your life, beside the last
groans of the dialysis machine,

and further into the bald insistence
of your pain, there is an old country.
There is a voice and a landscape.

Brother, whatever the first sin
we cultivated like a flower, whatever
our first address, whatever the blank page
of the one memory we bronzed over and over
like a first, tiny shoe. . .

Voice of the moth's turning, of ash
in bloom and your wrong blood, John,
your name is a held breath.
                              Under the earth,
your left hand is a map.

2. *His Birth*

Settled in, and waiting, the tiny ribs
nudge and bloom, having prepared for this.

The blue stub of each bone pushes
its way through its socket of milk
into its socket of bone. God's one elbow
bends, on cue.
                 John, already the dark
fevers take root toward you. Already
the marked days start sweating it out.
Already the day chill and the night chill.

Dropped child, Runge's wet dream,
it's all there in your name
fixed as the skin it hangs on.—

The white sky of belly is there.
And the veined lamps, the eyes, are there.
And the fine mesh of wrist, the miracle of toe,
is there, is there.

        Brother, we go back
and tug at the fire root, the snapped
yew branch before the field.

And then it happens, the womb
stirs like a startled tongue,
the wild oration of birth.

3. *Dialysis Machine*

This pulse is a brilliant noise,
a slow gurgle, the sound of phlegm
rising in a throat of sorrow; cold

lights wink and flash, the water pump
works its blood-load, scissor-clamps
gauge flow, ebb, offer deep directions—

heart to vinyl veins and back, out
of the broken body and back.

In this pure re-issuing of blood,
in the hum of metal and your breath,

you're anchored in, you're learning
the slow traffic of all time,
your sad immobility. *Brother,*

stasis is a healing. Our first
country is in it, and the one before that.

4. *Blood Clot*

Once more you lie down, acre of sleep
at your right side, acre of blood

scythed and picked clean at your left.
Once more you tuck the shunt arm under
your pocked chin, and the soft lids lower
back into their first posture
of sleep. . .

In the dream He is the red altar
I bend to He is the wood
I grind on my knees toward

                         His hands
are straw and release the white
mirror I find nothing in but mirror

The cells hold and the shunt swells,
the eighth factor of blood
doing time in its plastic sleeve

until mother's nightly glance
has her tearing the arm down, down,

the heparin worked in like a tar salve,
all of you muted again, flowing again.

5. *Adult Baptism*

Here are notions, strong airs, winds
you believe in: the low crack

of the knee of Grace, the slow
arm of Christ, flesh-colored candles
The Book of Acts was written by.

—Tokens of the faith, shards
of the heart's purity of heart.

And they all lead to this moment
of immersion, the sure breath of all
water pressed to your pink self.

Brother, I speak these words
to your sleep. Your mouth is watched.
Heaven is empty, and we're all in it,

singing the shapes of a few cornered things.

6. *Angel's Appearance*

You almost become her, and her breath of scars.
You almost learn her frayed syllables
of wine and direction, the full country
you dream of dying in.

                    John,
as she gives herself to the water fly,
as she holds herself still,
as she steadies your first breath

in her gnarled hand, you almost hear
the barbed tines of her song
reaching the date of your birth.

Brother, whose name is a lip of fire?
Where are the footprints of this tongue?
Who dropped the playing card on my fourth year?
Where are the graves opening like doors?

She looks on, approaching a harsh color.
She extends her regret like a blessing.

7. *Funeral Home*

This is a table that will not rise,
and this is a dust that will.

And this is your empty body,
laid out, rouged, absurd
amid the sweet fists of tulips.

(Perhaps it's a fevered equation,
this story-line pregnant with departure,
acts of a simple eye:

the beard you never shaved; your one
motion miss-set and stilled; your voice
tight as scissors rusted over years:

*The last sound I remember
was a nurse cursing. The last image
a commercial for bread. . .)*

And this is the sound of the grieving
father, a breath in your new silence.

8.

O *aletheia*, the sudden flickerings
of the dead, as they drop limb

by limb into the Kanawha River,
into the black nest of sun.

Tom, brother, your name too will take
its place among these roots; look,

there it is, tied to your wrist, staring
back at you like a white sin. . .

John, if you had fallen, if you
had been held up and let go,
but moved on anyway, your shape

a dropped chalice, your scars
a cold Host. . .

       John,
if you had made a final withdrawal,

which you have. . .

9.

It must be a country without pain;
it must be a quiet place where the stillness

under your wrist is entered like a field
of thyme and peppergrass, the sun
breaking out over a slight rise

of hills, the familiar burdens
of clouds keeping in touch.

And I think of your lifted features,
how I've hunted them all night
through the March dark, piecing

you back, and back, trying to take
what this landscape is giving me:

watered lawns, a well, and across
a two-lane highway, slow cows grazing
the black earth.
                   Brother, this

is the miracle: we began
alike, that man's secret
told, twice, to that woman.

II

Find your own answer.

—Leibniz, *Discourse on Metaphysics*

SONG OF A COUNTRY PRIEST

> "Naturally I keep
> my thoughts to myself."
> —Bernanos, *Diary of a Country Priest*

April 4. Wind hums
in the fireweed, the dogwood
drops white skirts across

the lawn. From this window
I've watched the pink shimmer
of morning light spread

to the sky and the blond
grass lift the dew. *You
in whose yet greater light,*

etc. My prayers grow
smaller each dawn. Each dawn
I wake to this landscape

of thyme, rue, a maple
whose roots are the highways
of ants, cattails down

to the river. I rise
and look and learn again:
I believe in my backyard.

I can mimic the sway
of weeds in wind. I can
study the patience

of tendrils. God knows what
I am, a rib of earth?
a hidden cloud? I am

old now. I am a priest
without believers. I counsel
leaves, fallen petals, two

bluejays and one shy wren.
In my book of Genesis,
the serpent says, "You can't

tempt me with green
peppers, yellow squash,
the ripe meats of Eden.

I'm looking under my
belly for the next meal.
I'm lying beside a dirt

road in West Virginia,
waiting for a pickup
to stir a thick cloud

of dust into my mouth.
I will never hunger.
I will live like this

forever—inching with
rhythm across the dried
dirt, pulling myself

like a white glove through
meal after parched, ecstatic
meal. . ."

Perhaps my blasphemies
have saved me. Perhaps God
reads between these lines,

that whiteness touched
by no one. I'm ready
for Him to settle my

body like an argument;
my ashes can settle
where they will. God could

fall like an evening sun
to say Eat dust
with the serpent, crawl

on your belly. He could
say the earth is a secret
told by quartz vein and

nothing else. Tonight
in the thin dark He could
whisper the sky is the

earth, the stars are foxgloves,
quince blossoms, white flames
of trilliums, and I am

flaring and vanishing
above them. I'm ready.
I would believe it all.

MAY I READ YOU A FEW LINES FROM PEPYS' DIARY?

The green is everywhere, over Hinksey Hill and Cumnor, through the path-lining trees of Addison's Walk, past stray deer and coughing cows, the full fern and leaves, and Greyhound Meadow on the River Cherwell, over which looms Magdalen Tower of Magdalen College, Oxford. A green greener than any particular.

*

Here, in gray stone walls overlooking this green, C. S. Lewis, the Christian Platonist, tutors, gives lectures, writes his letters, his sermons, his poems, his essays, presides over the Oxford Socratic Club and enjoys the verbal swordplay of his friends. *Opposition*, Barfield reminds him, *is true friendship*.

*

Rain and more rain on the cobblewalks. The drops pocking the ponds, singing on the lawns, the girl in the sunbonnet blue a study in the curious watershyness of Americans as she ducks the drops under the arched umbrella of a stranger. I beg your pardon! snorts the stranger. Bloody tourists.

*

Here he has thought to use Aquinas as an epigraph for the second chapter of his book on pain. Would not the tidbit from Scotus do? No. Aquinas it will be. *Nothing which implies contradiction falls under the omnipotence of God*. Here he has read in the mornings, cherishing the old, scorning the new, the new critics, the new novelists, the new poets.

> *I would like my love to die*
> *and the rain to be falling on the graveyard*
> *and on me walking the streets*
> *mourning the first and last to love me*

*

Chopin on the rickety piano. The Preludes. Mrs. Kirkpatrick of Great Bookham of Surrey playing. Waves make one kind of music on rocks and another on sand and I don't know which of the two I'd rather have. Young Jack Lewis sitting at a teakwood desk writing Arthur Greeves, friend and defender of the homely. Of *Tristam Shandy*: It gives you the impression of an escaped lunatic's conversation while chasing his hat on a windy day. . .

*

John Henry Cardinal Newman preached here. Church of St. Mary the Virgin, University Church. Lewis, reading glasses leaning into his broad nose, stands behind the pulpit, an absolutely attentive, overcrowded congregation before him. Outside, the autumnal red of the tall trees gleans the green of the lowcut lawns. He has stared through his windows in Magdalen at this red, this green, as he wrote these words. Looking now to the deer chewing cud on the grass, now to his notebook. And nothing, not even a gable or a spire, to remind me that I am in a town.

*

Twaddle, he says to a student. Occam's razor to Plato's beard. A connection every undergraduate knows, or is laughed at. Jack, initially disappointed with his students, came to expect not so much. Do you see, now, why this is twaddle? There is so much to see, to feel, to learn. No, sir, not yet I don't. The rain on the roof, like a distant cock's crowing. How can it be that the rain falls as the sun shines? Well now, Jack says. What are we to *do* with you?

*

An American reader writes him a long letter, in admiration for *The Discarded Image*. P. S. Are you the sibling of Wyndham Lewis, whom Eliot called more primitive yet more civilized than his contemporaries? Thank you indeed, Jack writes. My dear brother Warnie is, I'm afraid, every bit as primitive and as civilized as his contemporaries.

*

Memory in Augustine. A rooting out, sleuthing the soul and the past for the directive hand, God's fingerprint. *Christians are wrong, but all the rest are bores.* Jack raises a wine glass to his lips but does not drink. Show me, he says to his brother Warnie, this machine, this motorcycle. The rough road rises and dips, sears the countryside in two. A gold sun sets on the tilled green. When I set out I did not believe that Jesus Christ was the Son of God, but when we reached the zoo I did.

*

1914. A recurring dream. Philosophers, orderers and cataloguers of spirit. Rousseau, his face caked with powder and one black beauty mark beside the right flare of the nostril, looked lonely as a little boy in the front row, scratching his Circassian thigh. The Voltaire of Ferney, all skin and bone, his noggin tan from clearing land in the village, leaned across his aisle, bending the polite ear of Duns Scotus. The Ancients sat in wheelchairs in the rear of the room. Plato's golden body shone through his robe like light through wax paper. Pythagoras did wheelies in his wheelchair while Zeno proved admirably its impossibility, and Plotinus and Porphyry sat chitchatting about the Knower and the Known, the Intelligence, legs crossed like English gentlemen. Someone asked Kant to sit with the Greeks. Mein Gott! Kant cried, his delicate wrists and hands shaking. Mein Gott!

*

10 February 1927. A discussion as to whether God can understand his own necessity. Colin Hardie, Fellow of Magdalen and Tutor in Classics, found the *Summa* on a dust-caked shelf, searched through the index frantic as if being timed, and, not finding what he was after, his face aglow, said: He doesn't understand anything!

*

The genius of this world is the other world. Owen Barfield, Jack's friend for over forty years, strode walking tour after walking tour with him, their pipes puffing, a swirl of smoke their wake as they walked. Anthroposophy, Barfield was saying, and Goethe as scientist. Miles from the towers, the Bodleian, the sun-shot gothic spires, the students and the work to be done, the landscapes they see on these walks command the eye, the sky blowing through the willows and chestnut trees, the fields falling at their feet like wet towels. Nature, Jack says, has that in her which compels us to invent giants. And only giants will do. . .

FOUR PURGATORY POEMS

1

So many small flames
in the dim cathedral,
like a chorus
of high, wavering voices.

You add another, lighting
a candle for the doctor
whose life's work you are.

2

Something's not right. You can't place it;
you feel like that character in Kafka
whose feet never touched the ground, a simple
man hovering above the streets of Prague.

The day breaks, the sunlight rains down
all afternoon, but something's wrong. . .
It's as though you walked out of yourself.
It's as though the sky leaned a little closer.

It's as though your sorrow, like loose change,
slipped through a hole in your pocket. . .

3

. . . You see the one
unashamed of his listening,
unashamed that he rises
from his knees, the way others
rise from a meal: tired, serene,

his face emptied
and waiting
for the next hunger.

4

At a long table
you write out the story
of your failures
as the blank pages
turn blank again.

TRIPTYCH: AUGUSTINE OF HIPPO

1.

Memory in Augustine. A rooting out, sleuthing the soul and the past for
the directive hand, God's fingerprint.

We cannot hear the roots reach under bunch grass and thistle.

He wrote one poem in seventy-six years: a poem praising the limitations of
praise.

Words marry, listening to each other. Precise in their disregard of us.

As a child I was told the Holy Spirit was nice but the Holy Ghost was scary.

His poem as limit of a votive candle's flame.

Early May. White bursts on the mountain ash.

Loss as frayed syllables. What goes "through the long, twisting lanes of
speech" is not what comes out.

Bee-buzz carefully drowns out his sermons, sunlight dazzling the souls of
the lost.

An image of the city as sweet structure and matrix of assent.

And always the small stars overhead, or rain pocking the surface of pooled
water.

2.

To put man in
    his place:

Thagaste,
	354 A. D.

A world
	of farmers
'As a boy, he
	could only

imagine
	(and fear)
the sea by
	looking into

a glass of water'
	Like Tsarist
Russia—
	patroni

to whom one
	bowed
But he—'shielded
	from misery'

by father Patricius
	the family
in a bad way—
	he

like Aurelius:
	'I have come
through pursuit of
	literature

to live
	the life
of a nobleman'
	The scene

eternal:
    insane
inflation,
    taxation

and perpetual
    war
the poor
    flogged

to instill
    reverent
dread
    him watching

wondering
    How to become
a schoolmaster?
    I went to

Carthage
    where my soul
had ulcers
    Adeodatus, his son

with (unnamed!)
    concubine
born
    'the effect

is sobering
    and thus
recommended
    to young husbands'

Mother Monica:
    You may not

enter
        my house

as a heretic
        Manichee!
(& dump the small-
        boned slut

a 'she-clog'
        in progress
to God)
        Oh, mother. . .

12 years
        since Cicero's
Hortensius
        inspired me

to study philosophy
        but still I
postponed
        renunciation

of this world's
        joys
Bishop Ambrose suggests
        read

the Book of
        Isaiah—
incomprehensible!
        To Cassiciacum

and *otium liberale,*
        cultured retirement
clear Italian skies
        rhythm

of running
      water
in the bathhouse
      two cocks

fighting
      in morning light
clarity
      of distant Alps

and of mind
      'Believe Him
who said, Seek
      and ye shall

find: it is more
      self-evident
than the properties
      of numbers'

Oh but my pupils are
      blockheads!
Boy: is soul
      of centipede

in chopped-up portions?
      'No God
without discipline'
      Soon the world

will stop;
      Monica's last
breath, *You were
      a good son*

Adeodatus
      to follow

her
    soon

'It is not
    possible
to live
    sweetly

with the mind'
    The Catholics
of Hippo
    (work to set him free

from grief)
    desperate:
Donatists
    control the

countryside's
    ovens!
come,
    serve us

Years, years—
    accumulating
authority
    among Roman lawmen

a slow and
    bitter
emergence
    in the public

eye
    'the Church
rising over
    the Roman world

like a moon'
    & he under
a bishop's
    packload

of tedium
    Then Cold
War
    with Donatists—

how to punish
    heretics?
persecution, coercion
    useful

'God teaches
    by inconvenience'
(the Middle Ages
    listening)

we are
    committed
to *agon*,
    wrestling-match

with
    mystical
twaddle
    & Devil himself

410: Rome
    crushed
'like an olive
    in the press'

his own health
    failing;

sent to
      countryside

to convalesce—
      African sunlight
still 'Queen
      of all Colors

pouring down,
      down
over
      everything'

A mellowing
      with old age?
Increasingly
      I think

of the intimate
      wonders
of the human
      body

Still, 20
      years left
to put man in
      his place—

Pelagius,
      Julian
'wind-bags
      puffed-up

with pride'
      (the form
of the witch-hunt
      still workable)

No rest
        from fevers
infesting
        Christ's

Body
        & his own
There is
        indeed

some light
        in us
but let us
        walk fast

walk fast
        lest the
shadows
        fall.

3.

Dear Augustine,

we move
from hour to hour here,
quiet, unknowing; the days

explicit and obscure.
You are a part of this.

Unde hoc malum?—
your stern urgency.

                *

We have traveled the past, its brief
certainties.
Then whole years of seeing nothing.

You say, There is a memory beyond memory.
You say, We are sure lines in somebody's palm.

*

Word after word,

you turn our heads from the dark to the dark.

We take from you a radiance
we can almost bear.

—Maker of the dark feared hard,
and of the light more appealing,
prayer is useless. I pray to you.

PAUL CELAN

Travelers above us: vulture and star.
And you, your name: two knots
in the rope of your breath.

Are you asleep?
—There's No-one's voice again.

      *

You hear a murmur in the tubes in your throat,
you hear your slow drip in the urine sack,

you hear your heart
which fell to pieces in the surgeon's hands,
you hear it beating,

you hear me carving someone
else's name in your crutches.

      *

You, star-hard.
Words sought you out and brought you back.

Still, to the rose and its shadow
you say: nothing.
To the hush of an answer,
to the distance between us: nothing.

      *

Are you asleep?
—There's No-one's voice again.

      *

Flower, word of the blind.
Our look waters it.

In the name of the blood-coin,
the open vein, in the name
of the lonely witness,

there are unheard rivers
inside us. There are cathedrals
we never see.

*

You've fingered your death
like a bread crumb in your pocket.
You're taking it

out. You're placing it on your lip.

Are you asleep?
—There's No-one's voice again.

ANIMIST

You are my lovely daughter, he says
too slowly. You will listen to me.

*

His voice enters her room.
Then he follows it.

*

His voice. Outside, the sycamore flaying
itself—the sound is there like the sky.

*

He says I will clothe you, feed you.
It's a kind of agreement between us.

*

Roots make a sound, a root-voice.
Branch, bark and weed: voices.

*

He says you are my daughter. I am
your father. Do you understand?

*

A radiance in the plum tree. . . She says
he said to hush like a bike on the lawn.

*

When I look at the plums I am father and daughter.
He is unsafe and he will not be quiet.

AFTER BOBROWSKI

1

Blackbirds in the elder,
trilling, the crickets' voice
cuts a notch in the wall,
the flight of swallows
against rain, stars move

in the sky, in the hoarfrost,

when they bury me
under the roots
they'll hear:
he speaks
to the sand
filling his mouth—so the sand
will speak
the stone cry
the water
fly

2

To say, The trees the tree until
To say, Whose water-voice

To say, Fear, shining
To say, Dead is dead

To say, How long in the veins
To say, Whisper another

To say, Someone walked awhile if not longer

To say, The tower toward
To say, Blazing mouth

To say, Or the cedar woods
To say, Singing down

To say, Labyrinthine dance
To say, You or you

To say, Crumbling or a lozenge of

THINKING OF WALLACE STEVENS

Word for word, what the cicada says
is beyond him now. And the moonlight,
writing its blue notes
in the margins of everything . . .

*

Sunday evening. Night falls in the stilled suburbs
of Hartford. He's making a low sound. Under
his breath, he's muttering about the mangroves
and jasmines he has seen in Key West,

the bright exhaustion of stars, the lust
of the bougainvillea. Physical streets
of the physical town. Your ear swims in the sound.
It is like nothing, nothing you have heard.

*

The wind in Asia is and is not the wind
in Hartford, he says. The tongue
is an eye. The eye is an element. . .

Be with us, old, fancy man.

PRIVATE COLLECTION

1. *Miró*

I am a red moon staining
a bird's flight.

I am a spindly star and a breast
of mud.

I am the unknown's yellow hair.

I am a white glove in the blue
Majorcan sky.

I am a shimmer of orange at the edge
of your sight,

the black thread,
the thin black tail of the sun. . .

2. *Balthus*

You know that time of the day—
the sky grows the color of lake water,
the sun unseen and going down.

In such light,
I can barely make out her face,
can barely see her lips move
as she breathes in the dim room.

The sound when she stirs—
an arm pulled from a sleeve, an eraser
brushing these words.

No one can find her now.
She is asleep in this bed,
and the bed is empty.

3. *Dürer*

From the castle you can see
this barren wilderness:
not the lovely, ruined fields
of your childhood, but
deserted acres of shale stone,
packed clay, scattered weeds.
You will walk on all fours
in this place and study the ruts
of an ox-cart, crane up
at the sky. The precise
horizon-line always before you
like a tease of forgiveness. . .
You will crawl in shame for years
until from somewhere you hear
a rasping, the furious sucking
of a child at a woman's breast,
and look into the gentlest face
you will ever see, this woman
nursing her son. —The face
of the child like God's face,
ecstatic,
and utterly preoccupied. . .

4. *Chagall*

This is no drunkard's vision,
a dreamt-of, untouchable woman

freed from a sullen mind to
float like a dirigible above Vitebsk.

No, she is as fixed overhead
as the planets. Even

proper ladies have confessed
to her presence.

Children, in cruel
games, have named her:

Moonpie. Leg-of-Lamb.
In time they will come

to revere her. Only
travelers, passing through town

or catching sight in a train
window, are stunned, and unchanged.

But the townspeople shrug
their questions off. *Oh, you learn*

to live with her, they say.
And point to the sky

which has never turned
its face to them.

DR. FARNSWORTH, A CHIROPODIST, LIVED IN OHIO, WHERE HE WROTE ONLY THE FIRST LINES OF POEMS

1

The moon smells like a fishbone. The cow

2

Plotinus, Porphyry, strolling the lake's

3

1925. *Mountain, Table, Anchors, Navel*

4

The smell of God in wood.

5

"She came to him, nuzzling his chest."

6

Chaos in ochre. Time in the physical. Light

7

Past the barn, past the worm-ridden apple trees

8

Organ swell. Cadence. Swedenborg with a walking stick,

9

The sun, lost

10

I have never dreamed of water.

11

Will God work only in Geometry, Emerson

12

Say of me that I am living still.

POSTCARDS TO GÜNTER EICH

1 .

Persistent as lichen,
the world with its
sawhorse and vetch,
crowlight,
local accents.
Objects listen,
the roads are ice,
we cough and
are grateful.

2.

Blue iris,
intelligence in cities.
The grammar of the calendar.
Learning the habits
of my favorite wccd.
Translating what we saw
into what we saw.

3.

Hello, little eye.
I'm asking about
the inventions of leafmold,
October, syllables.
A nail. A sack.
Dialects everywhere
you look.

4.

I give you: a pear
Augustine might have stolen
as a youth. Quick,
read to me
of wicker chairs,
of cobwebs in far corners,
of a sadness
that isn't cheap.

5.

Towel and thread,
cup and spoon.
The names of things
in a far-off book.
Towel and thread,
cup and spoon.

III

the words
out of that whirlwind his
and not his strange
words surround him

—George Oppen, "The Tongues"

A LANGUAGE OF HEMOPHILIA

1

Blood pools in a joint
The limb locks

'Acute hemarthrosis'
'Thromboplastin generation'

Hear a language force
Intimacy with
Itself, the world

With and *of* as in skin's turning
Henna, oxblood, roan, russet

Bruise-blue, color of no jewel

'The secret is locked
        Inside
The structure
        Of the chromosomes'

2

hemo
philia

'blood'
'affection for'

trans
fusion

hema
toma

patho
genesis

anti
body

hyper
trophy

bio
assay

cry
cryo

precipitate
precipice

3

Achtung, says the world. Or was it you. The names of things in chalk on a blackboard. Stars narrow and go out like nothing. The dry in dry ice. The ice in it.

We grow what we can in this soil, some live in attics. The sea is a whale road, the sea is as coarsely gray as itself. Pronouns as 'accrued hieroglyph-ics.' Leaves take light in sympathy and greed.

Black paint for the swimmers and squirrels tightwalk the wire fence. He would spend a lifetime tracing each passage, each transgression of the word 'the.'

Local color. This is the sign of this. Words
spoken to no one, in particular.
"Those stories, dangerous

toxic waste in Richmond, AIDS discrimination, and celebrity hockey coming up." A friend said, "She seems to really care. For a hematologist, she seems really patient. Really personable."

Stars narrow and. The names of things in chalk
to the smaller Midwestern cities
quietly, as if ordered. Go out like nothing. His

sentence moved clockwise, 'native in native time.' Do you think it will rain. The sea. Black paint. Your eyes find work, there are forms to fill out. Whale road. Wire fence. Each breath

as it comes as it goes. Arterial
sunrise, capillary dusk. He wanted a listening
speech to approach all things with.

Do you think it will. "She made the disease very understandable and logical." "She explained all her words."

4

Ooze from a clot, ruined
Tissue

Do you think it will rain

The boy is wrenched from the womb with forceps causing a severe
        hematoma behind the back
Of the skull

Low sounds, the usual questions,
Selfishness transparent as a dog's

Aspirate the knee by extension the page

Firn, cyme, mere, hydrant, okra, bisque

Quoting Freud he said he was
Lived

5

'With these considerations in mind, the objectives of this Workshop on the Comprehensive Management of Musculoskeletal Disorders in Hemophilia can be stated briefly as outlined:

1. To bring together knowledgeable people in the field for the exchange of information;

2. To attempt to develop a commonly accepted system of management for the hemophilia patient with an orthopedic disability;

3. To develop lines of communication that would serve to foster clinical research in the field, thus leading to better methods of management;

4. To help disseminate currently available information regarding accepted methods of management through the publication of the proceedings of this workshop;

5. To encourage the development of additional centers of excellence for the management of the hemophiliac patient and his

6

problems.'

'All men

hate God'

—Melville.

I speak

to You, of

You, to

give

shape, shapes,

to both

of us.

7

Fibrinogen
Is going
Away now

Goodbye
Goodbye

8

Where like November

      back acolyte

the in

      ochre cedar rain

    *

Meadow

reshuffle

*

Rook bay mention

threading
           reading

dumb margueritte

*

The falls
           trillium

—singing, gray

blown cell

*

Goldfinch & wrist

           stiffened

splendid

           adjustments

*

Light light

pencil

           any more

*

Stutterer's

       door

mist   misted

       oh ash

       *

Inhear inhear

little eye

       *

Thin threshold

       again

or had

       so

9

The paramedic on the phone
Teaches; a teacher:

(Oppen: 'a substantial language
Of clarity, and of respect')

"Neck and wrists for Medicalert tag"

"Classical A or von Willebrand's"

"1714 Rolling Hills Circle"

10

'These child-
ren should
not

be
punished, and

their
play with
other

children
should

be super-

vised. If
possible,

they
should have
the

advantages of
a
warm,

dry

climate,

country
life,

and

sea
bath-

ing. Bleed-
ers

with
means

should take
up
some learn-

ed
profession

and, if
they

are
students, duel-

ing
should
be

for-
bidden.'

11

Somewhere,
            a name in chalk on a blackboard.

        *

Stars narrow staring into hills.

*

His sentence moved clockwise, 'native in native time.'

*

We grow what we can in this soil, some live in attics.

*

Window, sliding door.

*

He wanted a listening speech.

*

Arterial sunrise, capillary dusk.

*

Black paint for the swimmers and squirrels tightwalk the wire fence.

*

Will it rain he said.

*

Each breath as it comes as it goes.

*

A vine ascended the screen like a voice through a telephone.

*

"The sun will nickel and dime you to death."

*

"My solitude can lick your solitude any day of the week."

*

Wood, iron, stone.

*

As for pronouns: we're lucky to have them, like cobwebs or wasps.

*

He was given a 'battery' of tests.

*

Leaves take light tracing each passage, each transgression of the word 'the.'

*

Monday, Tuesday, Wednesday.

*

Do you think it will rain.

*

He would spend a lifetime listening like nothing.

*

Somewhere a name in chalk on a blackboard.

*

Firn, cyme, mere, hydrant, okra, bisque.

*

The boy is wrenched in sympathy and greed.

*

The rain he said the rain.

*

The error was mysterious and real.

*

"A word floored him."

*

Low sounds, the usual questions.

*

For a moment the world deferred but to what.

12

Mother said,
         What you say
     of Jesus
             Christ defines

you. End of
          discussion.
Thus I learned
          never to

speak of Him
          or desire
speech. But we
          had 'had words.'

One can break
          silence, but
make it, whole?
          'Diagnosis:

Hemoglobin—11.4 gm. per cent
RBC—4.6 million
Platelets—500,000
WBC—12, 850
Polys:
          Seg.—36
Lymphocytes—59
Monocytes—4
Eosinophiles—1

Coagulation Studies:

13

Clotting time—40 minutes (normal 5 to 10 minutes)
Clotting retraction—good
Prothrombin consumption—15.5 seconds (normal over 20 seconds)
Prothrombin time—17.5 seconds (control 14.5 seconds)
Recalcification time—8 minutes (normal less than 180 seconds)
Thromboplastin generation tests with the patient's plasma and serum and
alternately substituting normal plasma and serum confirmed the diagnosis
of classical hemophilia.'

14

"We read most of these words and numbers
Uncomprehendingly,
As if they were hieroglyphics"

A day, a day

Recurrences by which
'I' assume

'You'

Thistle, keyhole, spittle, crow

Glide, sample, knot, cheek

'In four years, 84 hemophiliacs have contracted AIDS and 56 have died. A
new test to screen donated blood for AIDS virus lowers the risk, but genet-
ically engineered factor VIII should carry no such risk at all and also be
much less expensive. Alan Brownstein, the head of the National Hemo-
philia Foundation, sees the race to produce it as "capitalism at its finest."'

Blood pools in a joint
Hear a language force
Firn, cyme, mere, hydrant

15

The boy pushes a fir twig
through an anthill, flattens
the small cone of dirt.

He studies the ants
escaping, their tiny
hysteria. They rush, weave,

turn and turn. The boy
looks. He looks. Words
are seen to intervene.

16

The weeds, he said, are reasonable here. What is the word for remember.
Listening objects. A low hum. A cry like a screendoor's.

What is the word to remember. He said the hospital is in that part of town
where German Shepherds have learned to pick locks, to sterilize a syringe.
Tell me something about yourself.

Phrases like 'river of wind.' To and fro. We do not know how the bread was
made. A grammar underfoot. He said a low deafening jet and was heard.

"She talked about hemophilia as if it were as ordinary as a cold."

Under the wood dock the catfish glide and vanish.

He said old so and so. To interpret the days of the week. Each accent was
local. Each an entrance.

What is the word. Unseasonable rains followed, a question of privacy. The
hills remain unread. He disagreed with his thought.

Posit water as water, the names in chalk. Listen, a friend said,

> 'I grew in green
> slide and slant
>   of shore and shade'

What for remember. Tell me about something yourself. Precipitate.
Precipice.

17

Possible articulate limb or look row after

row of you

18

Emboli
emboli

      *

Child
wren

finding

the
oak

      *

You, in a

radiance. You,

in a radiance.

19

'Speake that I may see thee.'

His question, when uttered, diminished. The back of his head in the clouds.

Crayfish, crabapple, stone's throw. What is a proper attention. Squirrels plump as squirrels, the sky seeded with light or not, as each word he read resembled itself, sandstone, hollyhock, membrane, beetroot. At least the likeness was striking.

His arm at rest while the plasma flows.

Or what is a listening speech.

There were parents who told horror stories about bleeding into the spine, into the kidney and liver. Staring into hills he finds a sentence singled out. Listening. Henna, oxblood, roan, russet. Into the throat and windpipe.

"His accomplished sleep"

Speake that I

Hushed have known

Window window

Finding the page

Emboli embodied

Threadbare ochre

Aspirate the knee to fully
Articulate

Wash the dirt from your hands and come to supper. Little eye, what is a word. To speak now of the room: the star-tiled floor, the straps and steel rails on the sides of the bed, the buzzer to the nurses' station, the television in the upper left-hand corner, the urinal and bedpan on the bedside table, the empty, 'immaculate' second bed.

"Uncover the story at the Museum of Natural History. I'm not an actor. We'll talk about how to control your anger. Start seeing motorcycles. I'm up to my ears in softness. You're right in the middle of it. Do you know what happens when you praise God. Listen to this. Try me. A powerful new reason. The freshness of pine. . . ."

You are as far / away / as that voice I / wanted / to speak to you / with.

Are the angers of the hospital those of the household.

Evening comes on. Stars flash and hang.

Once I watched a dialysis patient get up for the first time after a long illness.

20
Gratitude and
fear—Your relentless

rhythm—I move to
it still—How to

address with
care

whatever You are—

pooled
words, this
moment's cryo-

acquittal

NOTES

Some of the material for the poems about or addressed to writers is adapted from the work or biographies of those writers. The poem quoted in the fourth section of "May I Read You a Few Lines from Pepys' Diary?" is the fourth of Samuel Beckett's "Quatre Poèmes."

"May I Read You a Few Lines from Pepys' Diary?" is dedicated to Guy Davenport.

Robert and Suzanne Massie's book *Journey* (Knopf, 1975) has been an invaluable source of information and clarity regarding my own experience with hemophilia, and I have adapted material from it in "A Language of Hemophilia." Section 5 is taken from *Comprehensive Management of Musculoskeletal Disorders in Hemophilia* (National Academy of Sciences, 1973). The quotation in section 14 is from an article by Jerry E. Bishop published in *The Wall Street Journal* (July 25, 1985, Vol. LXV, No. 198). The lines quoted in section 16 are from Lorine Niedecker's poem, "Paean to Place."

"A Language of Hemophilia" is dedicated to Michael Cuddihy and Jack Ridl.

The Hemophiliac's Motorcycle

for Carrie

I

THE HEMOPHILIAC'S MOTORCYCLE

> For the sin against the HOLY GHOST is INGRATITUDE.
> —Christopher Smart, *Jubilate Agno*

May the Lord Jesus Christ bless the hemophiliac's motorcycle, the smell of knobby tires,

Bel-Ray oil mixed with gasoline, new brake and clutch cables and handlebar grips,

the whole bike smothered in WD40 (to prevent rust, and to make the bike shine),

may He divine that the complex smell that simplified my life was performing the work of the spirit,

a window into the net of gems, linkages below and behind the given material world,

my little corner of the world's danger and sweet risk, a hemophiliac dicing on motocross tracks

in Pennsylvania and Ohio and West Virginia each Sunday from April through November,

the raceway names to my mind then a perfect sensual music, Hidden Hills, Rocky Fork, Mt. Morris, Salt Creek,

and the tracks themselves part of that music, the double jumps and off-camber turns, whoop-de-doos and fifth-gear downhills,

and me with my jersey proclaiming my awkward faith—"Powered By Christ," it said above a silk-screened picture of a rider in a radical cross-up,

the bike flying sideways off a jump like a ramp, the rider leaning his whole body into a left-hand corner—

may He find His name glorified in such places and smells,

and in the people, Mike Bias, Charles Godby, Tracy Woods, David and Tommy Hill, Bill Schultz—

their names and faces snowing down to me now as I look upward to the past—

friends who taught me to look at the world luminously in front of my eyes,

to find for myself the right rhythm of wildness and precision, when to hold back and when to let go,

each of them with a style, a thumbprint, a way of tilting the bike this way or that out of a berm shot, or braking heavily into a corner,

may He hear a listening to the sure song of His will in those years,

for they flooded me with gratitude that His informing breath was breathed into me,

gratitude that His silence was the silence of all things, His presence palpable everywhere in his absence,

gratitude that the sun flashed on the Kanawha River, making it shimmer and wink,

gratitude that the river twisted like a wrist in its socket of bottomland, its water part of our speech

as my brother and I drifted in inner tubes fishing the Great White Carp,

gratitude that plump squirrels tight-walked telephone lines and trellises of honeysuckle vines

and swallows dove and banked through the limbs of sycamore trees, word-perfect and sun-stunned

in the middle of the afternoon, my infusion of factor VIII sucked in and
my brother's dialysis sucked in and out—

both of us bewildered by the body's deep swells and currents and eerie
backwaters,

our eyes widening at the white bursts on the mountain ash, at earthworms
inching into oil-rainbowed roads—

gratitude that the oak tops on the high hills beyond the lawns fingered the
denim sky

as cicadas drilled a shrill voice into the roadside sumac and peppergrass,

gratitude that after a rain catbirds crowded the damp air, bees spiraling
from one exploding blossom to another,

gratitude that at night the star clusters were like nun buoys moored to a
second sky, where God made room for us all,

may He adore each moment alive in the whirring world,

as now sitting up in this hospital bed brings a bright gladness for the
human body, membrane of web and dew

I want to hymn and abide by, splendor of tissue, splendor of cartilage and
bone,

splendor of the taillike spine's desire to stretch as it fills with blood

after a mundane backward plunge on an iced sidewalk in Ann Arbor,

splendor of fibrinogen and cryoprecipitate, loosening the blood pooled in
the stiffened joints

so I can sit up oh sit up in radiance, like speech after eight weeks of silence

and listen for Him in the blood-rush and clairvoyance of the healing body, in the sweet impersonal luck that keeps me now

from bleeding into the kidney or liver, or further into the spine,

listen for Him in the sound of my wife and my father weeping and rejoic-
ing,

listen as my mother kneels down on the tiled floor like Christopher Smart

praying with strangers on a cobbled London street, kneels here in broad
daylight

singing a "glorious hosanna from the den"

as nurses and orderlies and patients rolling their IV stands behind them
like luggage

stall and stare into the room and smile finally and shuffle off, having heard
God's great goodness lifted up

on my mother's tongue, each face transformed for a moment by ridicule

or sympathy before disappearing into the shunt-light of the hallway,

listen for Him in the snap and jerk of my roommate's curtain as he draws it
open

to look and look at my singing mother and her silent choir

and to wink at me with an understanding that passeth peace, this kind,
skeletal man

suffering from end-stage heart disease who loves science fiction and okra,

who on my first night here read aloud his grandson's bar mitzvah speech to
me,

". . . In my haftorah portion, the Lord takes Ezekiel to a valley full of
bones,

the Lord commands him to prophesy over the bones so they will become
people . . . ,"

and solemnly recited the entire text of the candlelighting ceremony,

"I would like to light the first candle in memory of Grandma Ruth, for
whom I was named,

I would like Grandma Dot and Grandpa Dan to come up and light the
second candle,

I would like Aunt Mary Ann and my Albuquerque cousins Alanna and Su-
sanna to come up and light the third candle . . . ,"

his voice rising steadily through the vinegary smell and brutal hush in the
room,

may the Lord hear our listening, His word like matchlight cupped to a
cigarette

the instant before the intake of breath, like the smoke clouds pooled in the
lit tobacco

before flooding the lungs and bloodstream, filtering into pith and marrow,

may He see Himself again in the hemophiliac's motorcycle

on a certain Sunday in 1975—Hidden Hills Raceway, Gallipolis, Ohio,

a first moto holeshot and wire-to-wire win, a miraculously benign side-
swipe early on in the second moto

bending the handlebars and front brake lever before the possessed rocket-
ing up through the pack

to finish third after passing Brian Kloser on his tricked-out Suzuki RM125

midair over the grandstand double jump—

may His absence arrive like that again here in this hygienic room,

not with the rush of a peaked power band and big air over the jumps

but with the strange intuitive calm of that race, a stillness somehow poised

in the body even as it pounded and blasted and held its line across the
washboard track,

may His silence plague us like that again,

may He bless our listening and our homely tongues.

II

AT BURT LAKE

To disappear into the right words
 and to be their meanings. . .

October dusk.
Pink scraps of clouds, a plum-colored sky.
The sycamore tree spills a few leaves.
The cold focuses like a lens. . .

Now night falls, its hair
caught in the lake's eye.

Such clarity of things. Already
I've said too much. . .

                      Lord,
language must happen to you
the way this black pane of water,
chipped and blistered with stars,
happens to me.

ARS POETICA

The dead drag a grappling hook for the living.
The hook is enormous. Suddenly it is tiny.
Suddenly one's voice is a small body falling
through silt and weeds, reaching wildly. . .

PRAYING WITH GEORGE HERBERT IN LATE WINTER

1

In fits and starts, Lord,
    our words work
the other side of language

where you lie if you can be said
    to lie. Mercy upon
the priest who calls on you

to nurture and to terrorize
    him, for you oblige.
Mercy upon you, breath's engine

returning what is to what is.
    Outside, light swarms
and particularizes the snow;

tree limbs crack with ice
    and drop. I can say
there is a larger something

inside me. I can say,
    "Gratitude is
a strange country." But what

would I give to live there?

2

    Something breaks in us,
and keeps breaking. Charity,
    be severe with me.
Mercy, lay on your hands.

White robes on
the cypress tree. Sparrows
            clot the fence posts;
they hop once and weave

            through the bleached air.
Lord, I drift on the words
            I speak to you—
the words take on

            and utter me. In what
language are you not
            what *we* say you are?
Surprise me, Lord, as a seed

            surprises itself. . .

3

    Today the sun has the inward look
of the eye of the Christ Child.
    Grace falls at odd angles from heaven

    to earth: my sins are bright sparks
in the dark of blamelessness. . .
    Yes. From my window I watch a boy step

    backwards down the snow-covered road,
studying his sudden boot tracks.
    The wedding of his look and the world!

    And for a moment, Lord, I think
I understand about you and silence. . .
    But what a racket I make in telling you.

A VISIT TO THE CATHEDRAL

After the sudden hush and cool
as the doors close,

after we inch into the north aisle
as though into a held breath,

after we cluster like bees around
the jeweled splinter of the True Cross,

I see another nave envelop the nave,
immense, borne up

by the buttresses and cross-ribbed vaults
of what you said to me just now.

READING FRANK O'HARA IN THE HOSPITAL

1

The IV drips its slow news.
So long, lean and turbulent morning!
I wonder if my roommate would swap

2

Schlegel's *Lucinde* for his scrambled eggs?
Each thing bears its gifts,
the power lines' birds settle and cry out:

3

"You too could be Premier of France,
if only. . .
if only. . ."

4

The lights
in here are so excitement prone!
but the sun is undefended. Doctor,

5

I feel like I'm rushing
toward you with an olive branch. . .
With my cheese sandwich and wrist tag,

6

 I could be six years old again—
look out, jungle gym! Now
outside I hear "a bulldozer in heat

7

stuck in mud." And the world
narrows to this window above
the hospital gift shop. No, it widens.

READING THE *TAO TE CHING* IN THE HOSPITAL

The ceiling closes in like an argument
then floats off, losing the thread. . .

The room listens. The room empties
its mind of me. *The more*

you speak of it, the less you understand.

A glass of water. The arrangement
of pills in a paper cup. The precise
folds of the pillowcase—

substantial as fear
or need. *Hold on to the center.*

To speak one word bright
with attention. To wait and wake
perpetually to the room's

anonymous plunge.

WHEN COMFORT ARRIVES

1

Are there comings and goings among the stars?
Who would look for signs this evening,

when the sky seems wrong from your small room
and the future appears as something forgotten?

You want to walk and keep walking,
tense steps toward an early home. . .

You think the crickets, the moonlight, are better
than you. When comfort arrives, how will you see it,

by what dark luggage? Your friends know.
Its speech, they say, is a listening;

its mercy is severe—
empty yourself, and again.

2

A selfless song is its own praise.
Mandelstam said that. Moments of splendor

seen from the other side of a chained door.
Goldfinch, lilac, pine forest. The spiderweb

of light. Death is no terrible height
you peer over now and then—

it's simple, a fine silence, rain on black
earth. You almost see him, waving his arms

in a blizzard and disappearing.
I want to give back this dust

I've borrowed, he wrote once. And later,
It's no longer me singing, it's my breath.

3

You're walking, disappearing into a stand of elms
at evening, the way thought disappears before sleep,

or the way your voice disappears and you hear,
suddenly, another's voice, blaming you. . .

The nonsense of crickets. The moon bleaches
the grass, the elms swell as a low wind lifts.

You want to know what your hands know,
gripping a cattail, picking a ripe pear.

Or what your breath knows, its rise and fall
a slow, steady song. It's late. Somewhere

your friends imagine the worst about you.
In fear for you, and in something like love.

4

The sky pitches its blue tent. A crisp day.
You wonder if you aren't here to interpret:

the smell of thyme in a neighbor's garden,
the wind with its gift of a strange tongue.

Cows graze on a hillside. They're not
overlooking you. Still, there is

always a bitter ache holding you back
from the pure joy of giving up. Always

a reason to seek God's lucid ear.
You watch a spider assemble the air

and a cardinal lifts from a branch in flame.
Sometimes you look for the world, and it's there.

5

The dead are articulate, and know what to say.
The dead are not destroyers.

So many stories clamoring for attention,
asking to be yours. . .

You think of Mandelstam, of the determined script
of the letters of your friends. Imagination

as bridge. On the other side of
understanding, a goldfinch is providing.

A time comes when you want to account for tears
and wrong silences, when the promises

you make to yourself
and to others are the same promises. . .

6

You're walking again, this time with a friend.
—Both of you curious, both of you

tongue-tied under the sure drift of the stars.
You're learning the patience it takes to stride

in time with another. You want to pull a few words
from your life, speak to this listening face:

Most everything I know doesn't matter.
The night sky is as brilliant as the day sky,

you think, a vast, black astonishment. . .
Most, your friend says. *You're here now. Are you cold?*

The wind. The thread of quiet. You want
what your friend wants. A careful, human voice.

7

We're always looking for some good advice,
and anyone who will listen to it.

Stand up and feel your stiff body steady itself.
Step from the porch and watch the light blow all over you.

Once, you left despair at a friend's door
like a child to be looked after.

Your friend said, *Tomorrow your life will matter
to us both*. You laughed, and slept.

There is no word for the stark gratitude
we feel for friends. Just more advice:

Take your own pulse once in a while.
Consider the ant, and be wise.

8

Driving to Petoskey, you pass struck raccoons,
avenues of pines, miles of stripped birch trees

rising like broken pencils from the hills
and thawing marshes. A red-tailed hawk hangs

like a speck of black soot in the rearview mirror.
This far north, summer inches up through the earth

like spring. You're learning the trick of the good
daydream: the quieting words, sure images

of failure trailed by possible love. Yes,
leave comfort root-room, and try to name it.—

The word you want to say is a little word,
just big enough for the sweat bee, the inchworm. . .

9

Vulture and star, hyacinth and sun. The patient
hats of Queen Anne's lace. Say everything,

everything witnesses. The tide edits the shore-
line and the first light primes the sky; say

morning invites your small talk. *Dew slips from
a fern. It will rain. Where are the trilliums?*

Here is a story. The sky hums, some dragonflies
pause over their shadows and dart off.

An awkward moment comes when you say, *This is
my life*. Earnestly, without regret. The trilliums

are gone, the tiny veins of new ferns fill with rain.
There is no substitute for a lifetime.

EVENING SONG

The crickets go on with their shrill music.
The sun drops down.

What was it my brother said to me once
in Charleston, before he disappeared that spring
like the quick wake of a water mite?

This was 1980, evening, the porch lights burning.
He was reading from *The Cloud of Unknowing*.

Robins gossiped in the poplars,
moths spiraled across the uncut grass.
Moonlight wormed through the neighboring lawns.

We must therefore pray . . . not in many words,
but in a little word of one syllable.

Didn't he say forgiveness was his homely double?
Didn't he say what I wanted him to say? Maybe
I wasn't listening, chewing a branch of sassafras. . .

But I doubt it. As I doubt, now, that the life
of my lawn is a still life, the moon and shrill chants

opinions on despair. There are times
when the sound the world makes is a little word.
Something like *help*, or *yes*. . .

III

HYMNING THE KANAWHA

1

         Day brings a steady
hand, a sure breath every other day. . .

My brother again on the edge of his bed,
sitting up with his eyes closed,
his palms pressed, a brief prayer.

     You see we're in trouble

Spring, 1972. The last flare
of an April dusk. Sure breaths and relief
after a run on dialysis. He's telling
an old story, his slim translations
of Psalms, to whoever is listening.

     Give us strength enough

The passionate calm after a run—
his pulse grows as the fresh blood thins,
his drugged face opens like a fist.

     *

Runnels of spring rain. Branches
like floating ribs from the camphor trees.

Someone is asking you to make a fist.
Someone is taking your pulse
and saying nothing, and starting to weep

over the jonquils and the yellow grass,
over the cold surge of the Kanawha River.

2

Slurs on the Psalms he calls these prayers.
And writes them out
in a notebook he keeps under his pillow,
and shows no one.

> *Death has fallen on me*
> *like a stone I can't budge*

> *Once death was my companion*
> *We walked together in your house*

It's an odd-numbered day,
the machine, like another child, bathed and asleep.

Before he sleeps tonight, my brother will forgive
his body anything—night sores, bad numbers,
pain like a word. . .

Before sleep, my brother will bless himself, and lie down.

*

The blood in a black widow falls asleep.

Near an almond branch,
work ants gather their meals in the noon sun.

At the far edge of a field, a hospital
is erected and torn down
on the same day, the healers now

working double time, now obsolete,
your failed kidneys swelling from pinholes

to buttonholes, buttonholes to large red sacks.

3

What's in the doctor's pause and the heart's,
the needle placed like a root
in the red vein. . .

The machine drones through the afternoon.
My parents shuffle about him, keeping the lines clean,
smoothing the blood's slow run from the body.

> *But I am no one*
> *I am poured out like water*

Scissor-clamps, the pump, coils: the hours
are counted out. Like coins, like yesterday's
good news, they pile up
just out of reach.

> *Lord, be near*

*

X rays of the hip joint, fat negatives,
milk-light your wronged bones.
For once you can hear yourself:

Syringe of sleep,
Syringe of another life,
close my eyes,
lift these white walls.

Your shadow ascends like a soul
from the stretcher but holds still.
In time, in good time, your own blood

mutters and wakes.

4

"Just to imagine
there is something larger than me, and purer."

Thus my brother, in a notebook, 1972.
A reason to rise in the long mornings.
Thus sun, moon, ghost-of-a-chance; what
the Psalms say.

> *How long will sorrow flow*
> *through my heart like bad blood*
> *How long will you be a stranger*
>
> *Like anyone*
> *I'm dying*

He writes at his desk, sure breath after
sure breath. Outside, the poplars; and I'm
spinning a ball through a netted hoop

over and over, getting better.

*

Reedstem, cattail, eyelash, a leaf. . .
A fine rain peppers the Kanawha, a cold
wind hustles the yew bushes and hollyhocks
in Tuendiewei Park. The log cabin there

rests on your fingertip, twilit; inside,
your grandparents parade in your white gowns,
their eyes the color of your eyes, their wake
the dust prints you'll leave behind.

5

There's a photograph, a boy on a beach, 1961.
My father took it. My brother
didn't know it. He sat on the hot sands,
tracing his noon shadow with a Lego stick.

Heat came in with the waves. He was five.
Morning opened up
like a torn fingernail, and began to bleed.
Eleven years. He sits under himself now, the flush
and pull of dialysis; writing sentences.

> *The river of God is full*
> *of water*

The edge of his straw hat casts a shadow
like gray fingers, water reeds. Gulls
tattooed the beach. At five, my brother saw

his shadow as a circle. Widening, opening.

*

The hallway goes out like a blown
candle, and you're back at your first house—

flies in the screen's light, white wings
fluttering through the grilled blackness.

You walk toward the coal cars by the riverbank:
damp smell of the cornfield at night;

over your head, the same stars
in their ordered slide. . .

Only this time it's wrong,
the face of the night nurse among the reeds

and birch branches, the whole landscape
caught like a moth in the renal room's dark.

6

Tonight, asleep, my brother walks
out into a mild rain on the driveway.
The pulse, he'll say, of drops collecting
into puddles is his pulse, the soft tick
against the windows his tick. . .

And tomorrow's an odd-numbered day,
nothing but sleep and a book.

> *a little sleep, a little folding*
> *of the hands*

My father goes out to bring him back
inside. He knows that he will keep this:
his son asleep in his pale flesh,

part of this rain and the black sky,
part of these black puddles filling the potholes
in the driveway.
                    (The hands ghostly, so steady. . .)

My brother is led to a dry bed, and lies down
whispering after a rain, the quiet
before a sleepwalker's footsteps. . .

          *

Your family, gathering themselves forever.

They play cards, or read, and wait for your step
and your suit of scars.
They stare past one another into

the river, and go on
waiting until your voice fills
the breezes again, until

the shine of the Kanawha
becomes their shine.

7

The machine drones like an old complaint.
My brother's shunt—a tubed sleeve, blood-vines
scaling the entire room, a red trellis
of veins. I'm eleven and looking on
for hours, as though over a roof's edge.

> *The peace of a good family*
> *like rare oil*
> *like your name*

We try to talk. Already, I know
the wrong words to say. I've rehearsed
the gestures of my hands, how fear
enters a child's voice. He's telling me
that it's all right, that if the mind
is lucid it can shine
like blown glass in a brilliant light. . .

His hands shake. His drugged face
blurs like a moon.

    *

You sit in a silence of rivers, the last

April driftings of the Kanawha, and watch
your own ashes being raised in wind

and scattered on the bank. Your family
looks on without a word. In a dry cove,
they've waited for your body to float by

like driftwood, for your one call
from the nettles, from the crickets' chirrs,
from the flash of fireflies low in the grass. . .

8

When God died my brother learned to sing.
When God died my brother slipped through the house
like wind, rustling his papers and spread sheets
before leaving under a door without a sound.

> *Lord, I look at the night sky*
> *and see your fingerprints*

> *What are we, almost you*
> *There's sheep oxen birds*
> *There's the sea there's the field*

> *through which we see your vital hands*

Scissor-clamps, the pump, coils. The hours
are counted out. But a sure breath fills
the planet, and another—what the Psalms say—

a sure breath, a steady hand, every other day.

*

Along the east bank of the Kanawha River,
your shadow swells to its own poise

and walks into the chigger bush, burrs
clinging like tiny scabs to the silhouette.

It finds the warm grass in Tuendiewei Park
and lies down. It considers your guilt

and lies down. It turns back to the Kanawha
and rises, and slides into the black water,

your body drifting across the white
bedsheets, a slow erasure of your name. . .

IV

CODEINE DIARY

On November 15, 1972—one week after Nixon was reelected—I clapped my hands for fourteen hours and thirty-one minutes. I was listed in *The Guinness Book of World Records*. I was eleven years old.

My record was published on page 449 of the 1974 edition of the Guinness Book, landlocked between the listings for "Largest Circus" and "Club Swinging," in the chapter entitled "Human Achievements":

> *Clapping.* The duration record for continuous clapping is 14 hours 31 minutes by Thomas C. Andrews (b. April 30, 1961) at Charleston, West Virginia on November 15, 1972. He sustained an average of 120 claps per minute and an audibility range of at least 100 yards.

*

I would like to feel a stirring in my knee, calf, and ankle: a signal that the blood pooled there is being absorbed at last and the joints are opening again, like a fist or a jonquil.

*

I make $12,500 a year. I work as a copy editor for *Mathematical Reviews*, a bibliographic journal for mathematicians, physicists, statisticians, logicians, historians and philosophers of mathematics. When Joyce said he wrote for an ideal reader suffering from an ideal insomnia, he might well have had our subscribers in mind. At least they seem to be up all night, reading, assaying, scribbling after absolutes in a language the clipped densities of which rival, on a good night, any passage from *Finnegans Wake*.

*

I would like to feel a stirring.

*

Today is Thursday.

*

I'm writing this from my bed at the University of Michigan Hospital. It is 3 a.m. It is the half-dark of hospitals at night. I have had an accident. I have been in an accident.

From my window I can make out the iced-over Huron River and a tennis court covered with a taut white sheet of snow.

*

Philadelphia Enquirer November 28, 1972
Martin Bormann Reported Alive in South America
Champions' Routes to Glory
. . . And sometimes champions have highly developed imaginations that ⊙ help them in their quest for glory. Tom Andrews, only 11, of Charleston, W.Va., applauded without interruption for 14 hours 31 minutes. His father, Ray, so attested in an affidavit he sent to *The Guinness Book of World Records*.

The National Tattler January 28, 1973
Boy Breaks Hand-Clapping Record
He Probably Never Will Applaud Anyone!

Dear Tom,

It was certainly nice to read that you have broken the world's record in clapping. Keep your Dad busy getting that affidavit recorded.

We used to enjoy seeing how your Dad recorded you and John in your annual picture for Christmas. The last few years we had lost contact.

Congratulations again. Everyone is very proud of you.

Sincerely,
The Ripley Fishers

National Enquirer September 9, 1973
Director Who Made 'South Pacific' Reveals He Was Mentally Ill for 28 Years
Twins Engaged, Married and Have Babies on Same Day
Smothering Sneezes Can Harm You, Warns Doctor
11-Year-Old Boy Claps 94,520 Times in 14 Hours 31 Minutes
Tom Andrews doesn't expect anybody to give him a hand for breaking a world record. Especially after clapping for himself an astounding 94,520 times!

"I just wanted to break a world record," grinned freckle-faced Tom, who lives with his parents in Charleston, W.Va.

Norris McWhirter, co-compiler of the Guinness Book, told the Enquirer: "We don't have many 11-year-olds in the Guinness Book. So this is quite a remarkable feat."

Dear Tom,

Try to come out if you can, but if you can't that's o.k. I can play till about 4:00 or 5:00. I hope you come out. Will you walk with me today? Circle   YES   NO

I think you are the nicest boy over in Rolling Hills. I'm going to try to get you something.

Love, Diane

PS. Write back if you want to. Don't let anybody else see this except Nan if you want to. Or Laura. I just showed Nan and Laura. Do you mind? Circle   YES   NO

Answer questions and give back, please.

*

"That your scrapbook?" Ellen, the night nurse, asks.

When I mutter that, technically, it's my mother's, who brought it to the hospital to cheer me up, Ellen glances at the *National Enquirer* headline and says, "You did that? Clapped your hands?"

I nod.

"Lord!" she says. "Did you have a major bleed, or what?"

*

Two days after my brother died I learned to juggle apples.

As children John and I stared in wonder at jugglers, at the blurred orbits of their hovering knives or bowling pins, at their taunting nonchalance. Gravity flowed from their fingers. Two days after John died, in Charleston for the funeral, I traced on notebook paper the looping flight paths three objects must follow to remain aloft while being shuttled from hand to hand. I was staying at my great-aunt's apartment on Kanawha Boulevard. She kept a bowl of fresh fruit on a coffee table in the living room, where I found three apples of serviceable size and with them made an inelegant leap from theory to practice. I kept dropping the same apple. Once it fell against a corner of the coffee table: the yellow skin split and juice began to drip. I dropped it again. More juice. And again. The smell was terrific, sweet as just-washed hair. Eventually I could keep all three bruised, dripping apples weaving in midair, circulating. Gravity flowed from my fingers.

*

I have had an accident.

*

I have had an accident on the sidewalk. I watched my feet come out from under me on the iced concrete with a kind of anecdotal perspective. The bleeding inside the joints, the infusions of factor VIII, the weeks of immobility, the waiting for codeine, the inventions with which my mind would veer in the direction of solid ground—as my weight drilled into the twisting leg I saw the whole pantomime emerge with the clarity of blown glass.

*

Sunrise. The sky gray and pink.

*

My roommate, an elderly man with end-stage heart disease, was rolled in on a stretcher today. Oxygen tubes curl around his ears, line his cheek, enter his nostrils. His wife reads newspapers while he sleeps. They look uncannily alike: white-haired, slight, their salmon-colored faces stretched tightly across the facial bones. He's yet to be awake in this room.

*

When I told my hematologist that as a teenager I had raced motocross, that in fact in one race in Gallipolis, Ohio, I had gotten the holeshot and was bumped in the first turn and run over by twenty-some motorcycles, she said, "No. Not with your factor level. I'm sorry, but you wouldn't withstand the head injuries. You like the sound of yourself being dramatic."

*

The riffled sea of my sheets.

*

There is a mathematical process, useful to physicists and probability theorists, called the "self-avoiding random walk." Walter, one of *MR*'s physics editors, once explained it to me as a succession of movements along a lattice of given dimensions, where the direction and length of each move is randomly determined, and where the walk does not return to a point already walked on. I almost wept with delight.

Walter looked confused. "You studied randomness in school?" he said, earnestly.

*

So many infusions of factor VIII. . .

As the concentrate filters into the IV drip, I feel the cold rise up through the upper arm, the shoulder, then branch off descending into the chest. I contain multitudes.

*

Heels clicking by in the hallway.

*

Later I learned that Walter would sometimes perform a kind of mime when he was drunk, a bodily interpretation of the self-avoiding random walk. Walter wore wire-rim glasses and a long, dazzlingly unkempt beard. He had close friends everywhere: Kyoto, Glasgow, Milan, Leningrad, Sao Paulo, Cape Town. I tried to imagine his self-avoidance. Head crooked severely, eyes fixed, doll-like, in the opposite direction, feet turned alternately inward and outward, arms flailing somehow along trajectories his head, eyes, and feet did not intersect. I liked Walter. He refused to publish a review of any paper that referred to "cone-shaped objects" and their velocity, heatseeking ability, etc.

*

In the hallway in the shunt-light
of the hallway
you wake
a nurse comes to show you
to your room
but can't find it
the entire wing is missing
you look outside
there in the gravel lot the sleet
pounding its fists
your white gown is walking home

*

Ellen takes the ice pack off my right calf and feels for a pulse at the ankle. She's been doing this every five minutes throughout the night to make sure the pressure of bleeding hasn't compressed and finally flattened the blood vessels. I'm a half hour or so into a dose of codeine: removing the ice pack doesn't make me cry out.

"It's still so hot," she says, meaning the skin around the calf. "You could fry an egg on it."

*

Glaring light. Shocking cold of the bedpan.

116

*

The President through the TV's drift and snow: "Things are even more like they are now than they've ever been."

*

Body positioning, weight distribution, throttle control.

Work with the bike. Don't fight it.

The sooner you shift your weight out of a corner, the sooner you can accelerate. Don't lose time between braking and accelerating.

Use the bike's ability to control itself.

Preparing the bike—the gear ratios, the suspension, the jetting—ahead of time will help your ability to concentrate on the race.

Concentration: don't let something stupid happen in the lulling middle of a race.

Adapt to the track as it changes. Be on the lookout for alternative lines.

Racing in the rain: controlled insanity. Get out front to avoid being roosted with mud from the rear tires of other riders.

*

There are times, in the last minutes before I am allowed, or allow myself, more codeine, when the pain inside the joints simplifies me utterly. I feel myself descending some kind of evolutionary ladder until I become as crude and guileless as an amoeba. The pain is not personal. I am incidental to it. It is like faith, the believer eclipsed by something immense. . .

*

You like the sound of yourself being dramatic.

*

Carrie's with me, often, during the day.

Her face. Her being here.

Our talks, and long easy silences.

*

"Does he have to do that?" the waitress at Pizza Hut asked. She passed out glasses of ice water from a tray, then set the tray down on the table.

"He's breaking a world record," John said flatly.

"Does it bother you?" my mother said. "I can't make him stop, but we can leave."

The waitress looked up. "You're joking, right? Let me see." She gestured for me to pull my hands out from under the table.

I showed my hands. Eyes, hostile, were staring from neighboring booths and tables.

"He has to sustain an audibility range of at least one hundred yards," John said.

"I'm getting the cook," she said. "He's got to see this."

A minute later a thin man with botched teeth, wearing a blue dough-smeared apron, was glaring at me. "Well," he said impatiently, "let's see your deal."

Again I showed my hands. I speeded up, just a little, the rate of clapping.

"Right. Unbelievable," the cook said, shaking his head and disappearing. I said, "Can we order?"

"What do you do if you have to go to the bathroom?" the waitress asked.

"I'd like a root beer," I said. "Do you have root beer?"

"He's trying to go the whole day without going," my mother said.

"Good luck!" the waitress said.

I said, "Do you have root beer?"

"Yeah, they have root beer," John said.

I said, "I was asking *her*, thank you very much."

"I don't think I could go the whole day," the waitress said. "I think I have a weak bladder."

I leaned over to John and whispered: "*Help*."

"Hey," said the waitress, "how are you going to eat pizza?"

"I'm not," I said. "I'm just sipping some root beer. If you have it."

"They have it, they have it," John said.

John buried his head in his hands.

"I'm going to feed him," my mother said.

"No way!" I said.

For a second I forgot to clap, then caught myself and reestablished my rhythm.

"We'll have a large mushroom and pepperoni," my mother said. "And I'd like a glass of iced tea. What do you want to drink?"

"I want a coke," John said.

"Root beer," I said.

*

Night. Snow falling past the window. It is codeine, breaking up and falling softly over the small field and train tracks, over the plowed roads, over the houses and apartment buildings, the river, the tall trees furred with ice.

*

When I was falling in love with Carrie, I wanted to astonish her with some simple devastating gesture, like the harmonica line in Neil Young's "Heart of Gold."

*

My roommate's lungs labor through sleep, each breath a furrow plowed in earth.

*

After the waitress left, my mother lectured me about not participating in events we scheduled on John's "off-days"—days when he wasn't on the dialysis machine. "You've known for a week that we were coming here. You could have picked another day for this clapping business." She said this in front of John, who grimaced and began looking around the room.

My argument was that just being there at Pizza Hut, while I was in the crucial early hours of breaking a world record, was sufficient participation, and that sipping a little root beer, under the circumstances, put me solidly in the off-day spirit of things.

She didn't see it that way.

I asked John what he thought. He shook his head; he wanted nothing to do with this conversation.

I kept clapping under the table. Later, after the waitress asked, giggling, if everything was all right with our pizza, I let my mother feed me a bite or two.

*

The sound of a dog barking ferociously.

*

There is a sleep like the long dissolve
of bone into brown dirt. The nurse carries
a paper cup, a syringe of that sleep. . .

But the chrysanthemums, and the trees outside
the window, say: *You are never tired enough.*

My second breath says it, and the room's tick,
the star-tiled floor, the chalk walls
through the night hours. I lie listening

as though to a voice inside my voice, a lullaby
deep in the throat. Now a small snowfall.
Now a first blur of sun staining the window.

*

Listening to Carrie's Walkman. A radio play from the fifties.
   "Hey, how'd you like a nice cool tall glass of water, chock-full of ice?"
   "Sounds great."
   "Well you're not going to get it you murderer!"

*

Dawn. Sunlight in defined rays through the clouds like spokes of a great wheel. There is a phrase for it. Yes. Sun dog.

*

I was elected to Phi Beta Kappa, graduated *summa cum laude* in philosophy, and went to work at 7-11. This was in 1984. 1 wasn't terribly well qualified, but I had worked at Sears when I was in high school and the manager needed a body behind the cash register pronto. So I got the job. When the matter of my hemophilia came up, the manager shrugged and said, "You shouldn't have any trouble. Unless somebody knocks you out or something."

I asked how often that was likely to happen.

"Hardly ever. Two months ago on the midnight shift a guy bashed my face in with a pistol butt. But that's really rare. If a guy holds you up, Southland wants you to give up the money. Don't be a hero. But since we just got hit up the odds are it won't happen again for, oh, eight months or so. It's the cycle of things."

*

Günter Eich wrote that "in each good line of poetry I hear the cane of the blindman striking: I am on secure ground now." Good or bad, each sentence I get down before the codeine wears off is a toehold toward equilibrium. Each phrase, quotation, memory, self-avoiding or not.

*

John, you're vague as mist, dressed up in dew, smoke. I keep seeing you, haunting the hawthorn trees within earshot of the riverbank. Asking nothing.

*

On Election Day I called my hematologist.

"Fourteen hours of clapping," she said, "could provoke a bleed in the palms, the wrists, in the muscles of the forearms. . ."

*

The days are perceptibly longer, lighter.

*

My leg shimmers, spreading its colors like a peacock: cinnabar, copper, rust, olive, ruddle, gentian, umber. . .

*

Brother, I always compare you
to a drifting log with iron nails in it
You float ashore   I pick you out on the beach
I'm building a small house with you

I always compare you to the sun
when the earth grows dark awhile
passing behind the clouds

*

I can see my heart beat through my hospital gown.

*

What surprised me was how easy it was to keep a precise and consistent rhythm. Two hours into the record, I felt as if my hands, like the legs of runners who have broken through the "wall," could hammer away at themselves effortlessly and indefinitely. At that point I knew I would not start a bleed. I had no doubt. And yet my hands kept hammering at themselves. Hammering.

*

Sometimes my roommate's breathing speeds up suddenly, like quick deep hits on a cigarette. This lasts only a few seconds.

*

"Nixon's problem is, he's not eating right," my mother said. "It's plain as day, anyone can see it. Just look at the man."

It was 5:30 p.m. and I was still at it, 120 claps per minute.

"Care for a drink?" my father said to himself. "Don't mind if I do, thank you for asking."

*

This morning I missed the plastic urinal, fouling the sheets.

*

The knee is locked at a forty-five-degree angle. Blood rushed the joint's interior, filled it, kept rushing. The muscles are shrinking to the shape of the bent leg.

"Straighten it as far as you comfortably can," says my hematologist. "But don't push it. What we want to avoid is another bleed inside the joint."

Yes. Yes.

*

A creekbed some goldenrod the tall
grasses arcing
over the flat field
you're walking a thin dirt path
the creek the faint rush of water
you watch your breath rise
like woodsmoke in first light
as a sudden memory
of ice across flesh returns the night
nurse saying *good morning*

*

Outside, snow's falling again. The loyal and fragmented snow.

*

This bed as embryonic world. Its vast cerulean distances, its equatorial thickets. Regions of hissing ash, monsoons, midnight suns. To move my leg a few inches: an emigration from Tashkent to Bogotá. To turn over: an impossible odyssey, a tale for Jules Verne.

*

Carrie tells me about a snowman children have built near our apartment. It's wearing Ray-Ban sunglasses and stereo headphones. I imagine the children at work on the torso. Snowball fights. Circling footprints. Their serious expressions, as if they'd just been reading the *Critique of Pure Reason*. The breath from their curses pluming in air.

*

She comes and goes, my hematologist. Sometimes a half dozen interns cluster around her. They look like children, rich white kids playing doctor, stethoscopes dangling absurdly from their gleaming necks.

*

Glancing through a galley set from *MR*, I find a paper—"Specification of an Algorithm for the Economizing of Memory"—with this: "An associative memory can be defined as a transformation between two sets. . . . This associative memory is shown to converge rapidly, and to have noise rejection properties and some learning capability."

*

Here, now

A pressure, a packed-in rawness in my back. Like a boot heel pressing down hard, but from inside the tissue out.

I'm pushing a hole through the buzzer to Ellen. A bruise in my thumb is nothing.

*

Hours in codeine's loose grip.

*

In the parking lot outside Pizza Hut John stepped on the heel of my shoe.
My heel popped out. "Flat tire?" John said.

I tried to slide back into my shoe without using my hands, which
clapped and clapped.

"Knock knock," John said.

"Who's there," I said.

My mother held the door to Pizza Hut open for us.

"Tom," he said.

"Forget it," I said. "Nothing doing."

*

X rays: thick smears of charcoal. I've bled into the muscles along the spinal
column. "If the bleeding becomes intraspinal," my hematologist says,
"paralysis is a not unlikely scenario." What can we do? "We can maintain,"
she says, "a factor VIII level of 40 to 50 percent for ten to fourteen days."

*

I turn my name over in my hand;
dull sleeve I slide in and out of

*

For a long time I asked John to come watch me race. Again and again he
refused. Finally he agreed to come to a race at Hidden Hills Raceway in
Gallipolis, Ohio—to shut me up, I think, as much as to satisfy his curios-
ity about his hemophiliac brother racing a motorcycle across the gouged
wilderness.

The road from Charleston to Gallipolis follows the Kanawha River
to Point Pleasant, where the Kanawha and the Ohio rivers converge in a
vast capital T sunk into bottomland. We passed coal barges drudging
through the black water, their wakes spreading across the width of the river
and lapping both banks. Before we got to Point Pleasant a heavy rain

started. Past Gallipolis, just past the farms and headquarters of Bob Evans Restaurants, we turned off the interstate onto a series of rain-slicked fireroads that led to the track. We were hauling: three times the pickup nearly slid off the road's shoulder. Eventually we pulled into the pit area at Hidden Hills. I wondered what John made of the scene. Riders tooling the pits with their helmets and shirts off, sideburned, thick arms tattooed and flexing. The smell of Bel-Ray oil and WD40. The ribbon of track snaking the Ohio landscape. Someone gunning a bike's motor; its spit and cough before going silent. He said nothing.

I knew John would have to wear a plastic bag over his shunt arm to keep the dust out. We were lucky it rained. Dust usually billowed wildly after the start of a race, a huge rolling wave breaking over the hills and shrouding the spectators. Rain would keep the dirt moist and on the track.

Midway through the practice sessions, however, the rain stopped. By the time of the first 125 moto, dust forced John into the cab of the pickup.

That is the image that attacks me now. John in the truck, windows rolled up, reading a book to pass the time while I kicked up the dust all around him.

*

An endless surge and drip of facts from the TV. . .

Israel is the most successful nation in the world in increasing rainfall artificially. . .

One billion years ago the sun was 20 to 30 percent dimmer. . .

Donald Duck received 291 votes in the Swedish election for prime minister. . .

Hang gliders in Los Angeles are using their bird's-eye view to help local police and fire departments. . .

*

This fierce inward stalking of patience.

*

I can feel the spinal muscles harden, filling with blood. I cannot straighten my back. The skin is boiling, sharp dots of heat along the spine like water in a pan. Or, alternately, an even heat just under the skin's surface, a steady flaming intensity.

*

"You have to imagine Richard Nixon as a little boy," my mother said. "A boy with a mother and a father, just like everybody else."

Now I tried to muffle the sound of my clapping.

"It's not that simple," my father said, "and you know it."

*

Carrie holding watch over me. Sadness visible in the folds of her wrinkled clothes.

*

In this morning's dream I was a clarinetist, giving a concert at DeVos Hall in Grand Rapids, soloing in a piece titled "Concerto for Clarinet and Cheese." It was poorly attended. At a certain point in the performance, the sound of my clarinet began to dwindle, as if a microphone were being turned down slowly. The baffled conductor stopped the orchestra. I played on. One could barely hear the melody by now, but the sound of the clarinet valves clicking open and shut was rising inexplicably through the concert hall, becoming a simultaneous music, underneath or alongside the blown notes, feeding them with staccato percussion. In this way the melody, slowly restored, and the clicking of the valves met as equals in the performance. . .

*

I can't shut out the sound of my roommate's breathing.

*

This morning my banana had a "Cholesterol Free" sticker on it.

*

Nine a.m. My mother and father arrive, emissaries from the mysterious sunlit world.

*

Random symmetries. . . Days when John's shunt clotted and he required I forget how many cc's of heparin to get his blood to stop coagulating.

Meanwhile, I'd start a bleed, and would need cryoprecipitate or factor VIII to get my blood to clot. . .

*

Tomorrow's forecast: "Just clouds."

*

More X rays. I've stopped bleeding into the spinal muscles. Soon enough, my hematologist says, my body will loosen and break down and absorb the hardened blood surrounding the spine, as it has been doing in my leg. There has been no intraspinal bleeding, no bleeding into the kidney or liver.

I look at Carrie. I look at my mother and father. We are inside a sudden astonishing calm. I seem to levitate and hover over the white sheets. . .

*

Once when John was dialyzing I tripped into the machine and jerked a tube clean out of its socket. John's blood pumped and sprayed into the air, splattering across the carpet and splotching our skin and clothes. My mother worked frantically to reconnect the tube and to stabilize John's blood pressure.

Later I noticed that some of the blood had seeped inside a picture frame on the wall beside the dialysis chair. The frame held a photograph of John and me wading in the Kanawha River, staring hard at the gray water.

128

*

Walking. Dew clings to the bunch grass.
The IV pushes a ghost needle back
into the vein. As I touch the bruises,

my eyes find work in the early sunlight,
my feet find their prints in the field.

NOTES

"The Hemophiliac's Motorcycle": The lines quoting haftorah and candle-lighting ceremony speeches were written by Ronald Kimball on the occasion of his bar mitzvah in Ann Arbor, Michigan, September 1988.

"When Comfort Arrives": Certain lines have been adapted or simply stolen without acknowledgment from the following. The seventh line of the sixth section is from Jack Ridl's poem, "In the Woods I Startled a Pheasant"; the last line of the seventh section is from Proverbs 6:6; the tenth line of the eighth section is from Hopkins's "My Own Heart Let Me More Have Pity On"; the last line of the poem is from Ezra Pound's 98th Canto. "When Comfort Arrives" is dedicated to Jack and Julie Ridl.

"Codeine Diary": The poem beginning "Brother, I always compare you. . ." is an adaptation of "The Mourning Song of Small-Lake-Underneath," from John R. Swanton's *Tlingit Myths and Texts* (Bureau of American Ethnology, 1909).

25 Short Films About Poetry

THE DEATH OF ALFRED, LORD TENNYSON

The camera pans a gorgeous snow-filled landscape: rolling hills, large black trees, a frozen river. The snow falls and falls. The camera stops to find Tennyson, in an armchair, in the middle of a snowy field.

Tennyson:
    It's snowing. The snow is like. . . the snow is like crushed aspirin,
    like bits of paper. . . no, it's like gauze bandages, clean teeth, shoelaces,
        headlights. . . no.
    I'm getting too old for this, it's like a huge T-shirt that's been chewed
        on by a dog,
    it's like semen, confetti, chalk, sea shells, woodsmoke, ash, soap, trillium, solitude, daydreaming. . . . Oh hell,
    you can see for yourself! That's what I hate about film!

He dies.

SIX ONE-LINE FILMSCRIPTS

Film Noir

Everyone on earth is asleep—except Robert Mitchum.

French Flick

The camera is an emptiness that longs to be a camera.

Historical Epic

Thousands of extras. . . reset their alarm clocks.

Stéphane Mallarmé Counts the Buttons on the Hangman's Vest

Mallarmé: Two, three. . . no. . . two. . . no. . . wait, two, three. . . one, two. . .

God, Guilt, and Death

This will not work on film.

The Needle

Medium shot of a camel squeezing through the eye of a needle.

DOVES AND FIRE

after a folk tale

Aerial shot of a small town engulfed in flames.

The flames, we see in a succession of close-ups, are as tall as storefronts, as tall as the town bank.

What most impresses us is their sound—a thunderous, deafening roar.

Shots of people clutching pets and photograph albums and clothing.

Now we see the flames approaching the town synagogue.

As the synagogue catches fire, a huge flock of white doves flies into and overwhelms the frame.

The wind generated by thousands of white doves flapping their wings extinguishes the fire. . .

SCENES FROM A MARRIAGE

Scene 1.

Rilke and Clara Westhoff on their honeymoon. Rilke is in bed, ill. Clara brings him some soup.

Rilke: Listen. I've written a poem for you. [*Reads:*]

> My fair dark lute, granted to me
> that I may test my mastery:
> Life itself I'll play on you!

Clara [*considering*]: Hmmmm.

Scene 2.

Months later. Clara is in the kitchen, chopping vegetables. Rilke sits at the kitchen table, writing.

Rilke [*reads*]:

> Perhaps we're here only to say
> death, in a hundred different ways . . .

Close-up of Clara rolling her eyes.

Rilke: What do you think, Clara? It's not finished, of course. Clara, did you hear?

She continues to chop vegetables.

Scene 3.

Later that evening. Rilke is still writing at the kitchen table. Clara is drying dishes.

Rilke: Here's another one, my sweet! [*Starts to read.*]

Clara [*throwing her dishtowel on the table*]: René, we need to set some ground rules.

Rilke: Brown rolls?

Clara: Ground rules!

Rilke: Oh. Actually, brown rolls sound pretty good about now. . .

Fade out.

THE RIVER OF BARNS

Wide-angle shot of a large river swollen with barns of all sizes in various stages of disintegration. Dusk. Crickets. A man and a woman walk by.

Man: How'd all those barns get in the river?
Woman: Beats me.

They watch the barns float and bob in the current for a while, then walk away. Fireflies flicker in the grass.

JACQUES DERRIDA AND GOD'S *TSIMTSUM*

An intensely exciting montage of Macchu Picchu, erupting volcanoes, North Pole glaciers, cells multiplying, Brazilian rainforests, E=MC², 200 MeV, undersea vistas, the Milky Way, etc., eventually leading us to the Mount of Olives, where God and Derrida loaf, the latter holding a Camcorder.

God: I withdraw Myself into Myself to provide a space and an occasion for all creation.

Derrida (*flustered, shaking the Camcorder*): Wait a minute. . . . Which button do I press? . . .

Videotape streams and spills out of the Camcorder. . . .

PORTRAIT OF A RED-HAIRED MAN

after Daniil Kharms

Fade in on a red-haired man.

The camera moves in until we see that the red-haired man has neither eyes nor ears. We also see that the man has no hair (thus he is called red-haired theoretically).

The camera continues: the man cannot speak, as he has no mouth. He cannot smell, as he has no nose.

The camera will not stop. The man has no arms or legs. He has no back, no spine, no internal organs. In fact, the man turns out not to exist at all.

It's best, therefore, if we don't pursue this film any further. . . .

THE PORNOGRAPHY OF CINEMA VÉRITÉ

1. Winter sunlight on a frozen pond.

Camera lens:
> The world is a naked body.
> That's the extent
> of my thinking about it.

2. Jorge Luis Borges on a park bench in Buenos Aires.

Borges:
> The camera speaks, yes, the camera says the naked world is (a) the
> Emperor's, (b) embalmed, (c) tame, (d) rife with pigs, (e) a siren,
> (f) fabulous, (g) rife with stray dogs, (h) included in many classifi-
> cations, (i) frenzied, (j) innumerable, (k) drawn with a very fine
> camelhair brush, (l) et cetera, (m) rife with just broken water
> pitchers, (n) confused, from a long way off, with a swarm of flies.

3. Winter sunlight on a frozen pond.

Camera lens:
> I still
> don't want to think about it!

RABELAIS IN THE HISTORY OF ABUSE

*Fade in on an immense field of cornflowers. Bright summer. We read "Near
La Rochelle, France, 1532."*

*Wide shot of a large man, holding a butterfly net, chasing a butterfly in
the field. The camera closes in until we see it is François Rabelais. He lunges at
the butterfly—lunges, stumbles, runs, turns, lunges again. . . .*

Rabelais:
>You jeering waif,
>you hinge without a door,
>sky's riffraff,
>split scrap
>of cloud fluff and worm paste,
>coxcomb strutting between
>bloodwort and heaven,
>carrot-colored
>lout, fop, boob, goosecap, loggerhead. . .

The film catches on fire; large hailstones fall on the audience.

INTERMISSION:
THE DISCREET CHARM OF UNFILMABLE FILMS

"Forget the novel," the poet Gregory Orr once remarked; "it's the movies that ruined poetry."

He was only half joking. After all, movies, as Fredric Jameson puts it in his fascinating study of film, *Signatures of the Visible*, "are a physical experience, and are remembered as such, stored up in bodily synapses that evade the thinking mind." How similar that sounds to the physical resonances that poets from Hopkins and Dickinson to Hall and Levertov have posited for their art. But where such poets were articulating a desire, an ambition for their poems, Jameson was simply stating a fact. Movies cannot help but be perceived synaptically, as it were; cannot help having the status of "first-order" experience. That kind of visceral response, Jameson says, "can happen with books, if the words are sensory enough; but it always happens with films. . . ." In other words, even the corniest, most shopworn Hollywood production, even the umpteenth remake of *King Solomon's Mines*, is "stored up in bodily synapses" in a way that only the best poems are. *It always happens with films.* No wonder some poets get testy at the thought of film's extravagant ascension.

That's one way of looking at it. Another is that of the French Surrealists, who originally saw in film an ideal medium for many of their objectives: the disruption of habitual narrative expectations, the introduction of the dream state, the embracing of the illogical and the inexplicable. As Philippe Soupault wrote,

> For us the cinema was an extraordinary discovery, and it coincided with our earliest formulations of surrealism. . . . We thought film a marvelous mode of expression for the dream state. . . . I myself believed it was possible to transpose surrealism to the screen because I considered the cinema a marvelous instrument through which one could achieve a form of surrealist poetry.

The cinema's darkness, Robert Desnos echoed, "was like that of our bedrooms before we went to sleep. The screen, we thought, might be equal to our dreams."

But with a few notable exceptions, the Surrealists' hopes for the cinema never materialized. Breton, looking back at the early days of the movement, noted that the Surrealists had made "parsimonious use" of film. This is hardly surprising; think of Breton or Péret working with a film production company! When I try to imagine such a collision I think of an encounter Pauline Kael describes in *Kiss Kiss Bang Bang*:

> Early this, year a producer-writer who began by goading me with lucrative offers—first to ghostwrite a book for him on "a sensational idea" (which turned out to be a denunciation of Method acting), then to work up a treatment for him on "an exciting new idea" (which turned out to be a spy spoof with a female spy), and then to do a quick (three week) rewrite on a script he'd had sitting around for a decade—became rather hurt that I didn't rise to the bait. Puzzled at my refusals, he asked, "Don't you want to do something creative?"

Cast Breton or Péret—or any of the Surrealists—in the role of Pauline Kael here and we begin to understand, I think, why the French film industry and the Surrealists did not rush to each other with open arms. (Richard Abel, in *French Cinema: The First Wave, 1915-1929*, gives a detailed account of other conditions of the French film industry at the end of the war that made Surrealist films unlikely to be produced. Such conditions included the "lack of capital for film production. . . the lag in advanced technological resources. . . [and] the loss of exhibition markets and of control over those even in France. . . .")

Failure is an opportunity, says Lao-tzu. And the "failure" of the Surrealists to get their films produced led to a marvelous invention: the unfilmable filmscript. Soupault's "cinematographic poems" (1917) may have been the first of their kind, but the excitement generated by the birth of a new genre lasted for at least a decade. In 1928 Benjamin Fondane declared, in the preface to his *Trois Scenarii—Ciné-poèmes*, "So let's kick off the era of unfilmable scenarios." Here is an excerpt from one of Fondane's scenarios, titled "Paupières mures" ("ripe eyelids"):

> 136 she puts him in her hand, looks at him: he becomes by
> turns

137   a marmoset
138   which she caresses
139   a phonograph
140   whose crank she turns
141   a begonia blossom
142   which she puts into her buttonhole
143   the young man looks at her, smiles with happiness
144   he becomes a glass jar in which red fish are swimming
145   the begonia blossom becomes a mouse

Each number represents an imaginary camera shot. The result is rather like a Péret poem with numbers assigned to each line: we see a similar play of invention, similarly abrupt metamorphoses and juxtapositions, a similar improvisational impulse.

As often happens, once I knew to look for unfilmable scenarios, they appeared everywhere: in the work of most of the Surrealists, in Federico García Lorca, in Helmut Heissenbüttel and Ilse Aichinger, in Barbara Guest and Kenneth Koch and many, many others. Lorca's "Buster Keaton's Outing," written in 1925, is a good introduction to the pleasures of such scenarios. Lorca's script is an homage to Buster Keaton's antic and straight-faced shenanigans, with darkly surreal twists (as when Keaton murders four children with a wooden dagger), and it includes some of the most deliciously unfilmable directions ever written. Of Buster Keaton's bicycle, for example, Lorca writes:

> *The landscape shrinks between the wheels of the Machine. The bicycle has only one dimension. It can fit inside books and lie flat in the bread oven. Buster Keaton's bicycle does not have a caramel seat and pedals of sugar, as evil men might wish. It is a bicycle like any other, except that it is the only one steeped in innocence. Adam and Eve would recoil in fright if they saw a glass of water; on the other hand, they would caress Keaton's bicycle.*

Surely even Tim Burton would throw up his hands at this point in the script. . . .

I first ran across these filmscripts shortly after finishing my second book of poems. My first two books were rather serious and elegiac; they dealt, for the most part, with my brother's experience with, and eventual death due to, kidney disease, and with my own experience with hemophilia. After finishing my second book, I knew I wanted to pursue a different impulse. I had always loved and admired writers like Sterne, Rabelais, Flann O'Brien and others who wrote out of an undogmatic, comic sense of the world. I knew that I wanted to pay homage to that sensibility, but I wasn't sure how to go about it. Shortly after I stumbled upon Soupault's "cinematographic poems" (I think it was while looking through old issues of *Transition*), Stuart Friebert, an editor of *FIELD*, suggested I try writing prose poems. As soon as I heard the suggestion, I knew the filmscript would be my particular entrance into the homage I hoped to write. Kenneth Koch's *One Thousand Avant-Garde Plays*, it is perhaps too obvious to mention, helped me find the form for the first filmscripts I wrote, for which I am very grateful.

One reason these scripts have been so much fun to work on is that they set up different expectations in the reader than do poems or stories or essays. Though they obviously need to be *read*, their effects are, the writer hopes, cinematic. That is, they require a reader's familiarity with the conventions of film. The writer also hopes to tap into the reader's physical experience and memory of movies, of the way movies are "stored up in bodily synapses that elude the thinking mind." Poets have been doing this implicitly for some time now, of course. Is it possible to imagine approaching the work of, say, John Ashbery or Leslie Scalapino or Charles Wright (to mention three very different poets) without ever having seen any movies? For that matter, imagine two early readers of *The Waste Land* and *The Cantos*—one a lover of movies, the other never having seen a single frame of moving film. What different poems they would have read! The writer of an "unfilmable scenario" simply makes explicit his or her debt to, and delight in, cinematic techniques.

I see a double bonus for the writer in this relationship with the reader. On the one hand unfilmable scenarios demand and acknowledge a certain sophistication on the reader's part. On the other hand they capitalize on our gullibility, the greater generosity we bring to the movies. As Jorge Luis Borges, an inveterate filmgoer, once said, "At the movies, we're all readers of Madame Delly" (Madame Delly being a sort of turn-of-the-century French precursor of Danielle Steel). Many of our most cherished aesthetic principles remain in the lobby when we go to the movies. By contrast, when we read poems, we tend to read in a spirit articulated by Donald Hall: "*No poem is so great as we demand that poetry be.*" As I say, the unfilmable scenario seems to negotiate an interesting middle ground between the gullible viewer/reader in us and the demanding one. Perhaps that negotiation can nudge both writer and reader into alertness for the conspicuous omission described by Barthelme's narrator in "The Film":

> Truth! That is another thing they said our film wouldn't contain. I had simply forgotten about it, in contemplating the series of triumphs that is my private life.

INSTRUCTIONS TO THE DIRECTOR OF AN UNFILMABLE FILM

This film consists of eighteen shots.

The first shot is like a set of propositions leading to an inexorable conclusion.

The second shot is like a name overheard in a restaurant.

The third shot is like the pendulum of a clock.

The fourth shot is like someone laying hands on you.

The fifth shot is like swimming in the open sea and remembering you have to make a telephone call.

The sixth shot is like learning the multiplication tables.

The seventh shot is like a vantage point high over a river and its valley.

The eighth shot is like the color orange.

The ninth shot is like an impatient doctor.

The tenth shot is like a refusal to be allowed entrance into an apartment building.

The eleventh shot is like a sudden precipice.

The twelfth shot is like hearing your own voice played back on a machine.

The thirteenth shot is like entering a church twenty minutes into the service.

The fourteenth shot is like sleep.

The fifteenth shot is like deciding to remain silent during a family squabble.

The sixteenth shot is like another set of propositions leading to another inexorable conclusion.

The seventeenth shot is like waking in the middle of the night to find the house empty, with all the lights on.

The eighteenth shot is like the first glance at a mirror after getting a haircut.

JOYCE KILMER, IN PICARDY, WORRIES ABOUT PLAGIARISM IN "TREES"

1. *Black screen. We read "June 1918" to the first bars of Henry Purcell's "They That Go Down To the Sea in Ships."*

2. *Cut to a bombed-out orchard. Deep trenches, barbed wire in coils, dissevered trees, wounded and dead soldiers lying about. . . .*

3. *The camera closes in on Joyce Kilmer and Soldier, their backs against the wall of a trench. We see other soldiers in the trench, some resting, some poised to fire. Gunfire. Silence.*

4. Joyce Kilmer:
   "I never saw a Purple Cow."
   Do you know that line, Soldier,
   from Gelett Burgess? Don't you think
   I have *adapted* rather than stolen it?
   Soldier?

Soldier:
   Right, Sergeant!

5. *Thunder of artillery. Joyce Kilmer pulls a book from his pocket and easily finds a certain page.*

6. *Close-up of the book:* Labour and Childhood *by Margaret McMillan.*

7. Joyce Kilmer [*reading*]:
   "Apparatus can be made by fools,
   but only God can make a tree."
   Now, wouldn't you say that
   even though it may *sound* remarkably similar. . .

8. *Nearby explosion. Dirt and dust flying.*

9. Soldier:
   Yessir!

BROODING KILMER, A DOCUMENTARY

Close-up of the cover of the August 1913 issue of Poetry: A Magazine of Verse, *framed against a backdrop of blue sky and fast-moving clouds. The magazine opens itself to "Trees." Slowly the camera moves toward the poem: when we are too close to take in the whole poem, the camera focuses on single lines, then on word clusters, then on single words. By the end we see only isolated letters and punctuation marks chosen at random. Occasionally we cut to Joyce Kilmer sitting in a dark room, chain-smoking.*

Joyce Kilmer:
> I am nothing, and I should be everything.

> *Pause.*

> What would happen to me if I stopped finding fault with myself, as I've been taught to do, and blamed everything on the state?

> *Pause.*

> Everyone's walking on a tightrope with their eyes closed.

> *Pause.*

> Money. More of it right away, and more of it in the future.

> *Pause.*

> In the end there is nothing that is not the case. Who ever said that?

> *Pause.*

> Winston Churchill was a hero of the electronic revolution, but also its victim. When his voice was no longer heard on the radio, it was as if he had vanished with a switch of the control knob.

> *Pause.*

Money is thinking through me.

Pause.

Money gives a certain unity to the world.

Pause.

I once said that the most elegant solution of the problem of opera was to blow up the opera houses, and I still think this true.

Blackout.

WILLIAM MAKEPEACE THACKERAY FOLLOWS HIS BLISS

The Fairfield County Fair in Lancaster, Ohio. Shots of Thackeray on the Ferris Wheel, the bumper cars, at the livestock auction, drinking beer at the demolition derby. Cut to Thackeray at the concession stand.

Thackeray: I can't make up my mind between Elephant Ears and a chili dog.

Concessionaire: Oh, go ahead, Mr. Thackeray, get both. You deserve it.

Thackeray: You're right. What the hell, Elephant Ears and chili dogs for everyone! They're on me!

Assembled passersby (*in chorus*): Oh boy! Thank you, William Makepeace Thackeray, possessor of one of the strangest middle names in history!

The fair comes to a halt as Thackeray is lifted and carried through the streets of Lancaster. . . .

THE MARBLE

Pitch dark. Feed in just enough light to make out the heavily-shadowed face of a man in his seventies staring at the camera. He appears nervous.

Man:

> Our Father in heaven,
>> hallowed be your name.
> May your kingdom come,
>> may your will be done
>> on earth as it is in heaven.
> Give us this day our daily bread,
>> and forgive us our sins,
>> as we forgive those who have sinned against us.
> And do not lead us into temptation,
>> but deliver us from evil.

Silence. With startling clarity we hear the sound of a marble rolling down a long, slight incline. Silence. The man looks around in the dark. Again the sound of the marble. This time it does not stop. Into the dark the man looks and looks. . . .

LECTURE ON SNOW

Winter snowstorm.

Long shot of an abandoned gas station in rural Ohio.

Beyond the gas station we can make out a road, fields, telephone wires, gray sky. . . .

Meanwhile a voice lectures on the intricate geometry of hydrogen atoms.

An old man huddled in an overcoat walks into the frame, tripping over the cement island which once housed the gas pumps. He falls and does not get up.

The voice continues.

Snow falls on the old man, the voice falls on the old man until he is a mound of snow in the abandoned station like a gas pump fallen over. . . . No: like an old man covered with snow. . . .

BATTLE FOR THE PLANET OF LAURENCE STERNE

A bowling green near London.

Laurence Sterne, Pantagruel, Sancho Panza, and Tom Andrews gallop on enormous hobby-horses, enacting scenes from the War of the Spanish Succession. Battle sounds. The camera shifts abruptly from close-ups of the legs of the hobby-horses to the riders' faces to views of the bowling green seen from a great distance. Throughout, the riders fall off their hobby-horses frequently and remount.

Pantagruel:
> Look—my horse! (*He falls.*) Ummph!

Tom Andrews (*shrugs, unimpressed*):
> Big deal. It's changing color. (*He falls.*) Christ!

Laurence Sterne:
> No kidding, it's like *The Wizard of Oz.* (*He lurches forward and almost falls.*) Whoa, boy! Steady. . . . By the way, want to know how they changed the horse's color in the movie?

Sancho Panza (*struggling, then falling*):
> Powdered Jell-O. They covered the horse with different shades of powdered Jell-O.

Laurence Sterne (*to the camera*):
> You can't tell that guy anything.

A sentry arrives on a real horse, with news of the Peace of Utrecht. All dismount, lugubriously, to Erik Satie's "Gymnopédies III."

THE MYSTERIOUS DISAPPEARANCE OF LAURENCE STERNE

We see newspapers spinning against a black backdrop as we hear Bernard Herrmann's music from Psycho. *The newspapers stop spinning long enough for us to read each headline in turn:*

WHERE IS LAURENCE STERNE?

BRIT NOVELIST REPORTED MISSING

SEARCH FOR STERNE CONTINUES

AUTHOR OF TRISTAM SHANDY FEARED DEAD

FOUL PLAY SUSPECTED IN STERNE DISAPPEARANCE

Cut to a map of the world, crisscrossed by a piece of string that we watch being pulled slowly by a toy airplane. Cut to Walter Winchell at a microphone.

Walter Winchell:
> Around the world people are asking the question: what happened to Laurence Sterne? Well, I have message for the goons who nabbed him. Goons, if you're listening, and I'll bet you are, J. Edgar Hoover and this reporter are on to you.

Cut to a montage of people listening to their radios: in bars, living rooms, offices, hospitals, a fire station, construction workers huddled around an old portable, etc. Cut to:

Walter Winchell:
> That's right, goons. Goons, you hear? I know you're out there. I know you're there. I know. . .

Iris in on Walter Winchell's mouth. Fade out.

THE MEXICAN JUMPING BEAN'S WILL

Fade in on a large city at dawn. Silence. Cut to a death-bed scene in the bedroom of a small apartment.

Mexican jumping bean:
     I leave
     my larva to the Pope,
     my chrysalis to the Cardinals,
     my molting to the Choir of Angels.
     Now I'm ready. Goodbye.

Fade out.

CINEMA VÉRITÉ: THE EMBRACE

On the screen we read, one at a time, one hundred verbs for bodily torture. After the first ten or so a solemn voice begins reading the verbs aloud. Soon the voice seems to be reading from a different list. The disparity between the voice and the verbs on the screen grows until the voice includes words (not only verbs) from entirely different subject areas. We hear, for instance, POWDERED MILK while reading CLAW; WATER TOWER while reading FLAY; and so on. At every tenth verb we cut very briefly to a couple on a picnic.

After one hundred verbs we see the couple embrace wordlessly.

No music.

CINEMA VÉRITÉ: WILLIAM WORDSWORTH REJECTS THE SPIRIT OF CARNIVAL

An old vaudeville theater, empty but for a few scattered men and women and a handful of actors and stagehands. William Wordsworth is alone on stage.

William Wordsworth [*reading*]:
                "What a shock
    For eyes and ears! what anarchy and din,
    Barbarian and infernal,—a phantasm,
    Monstrous in colour, motion, shape, sight, sound!"
    . . . blah, blah, blah—let me skip a bit here—
    "All movables of wonder, from all parts,
    Are here—Albinos, painted Indians, Dwarfs,
    The Horse of Knowledge, and the learned Pig,
    The Stone-eater, the man that swallows fire,
    Giants, Ventriloquists, the Invisible Girl,
    The Bust that speaks and moves its goggling eyes. . ."

A large hook appears from stage right and finds Wordsworth's neck, pulling him off stage. A voice (James Mason's?) reads The Prelude *in its entirety. Global warming occurs.*

FILM BEGINNING WITH A LINE BY ROBERTO JUARROZ

A net of looking holds the world together. Meanwhile the world, a little embarrassed, squirms to free itself. But the net's threads are too strong. They stretch briefly but will not break or yield. . . .

The camera, however, cannot see itself. Nor can the eye. Relentless montage of tulips, smokestacks, brooms, pickup trucks, coins, your body, dear reader, your gaze. . . .

This will not work on film.

A MAP IS NOT A TERRITORY

in memoriam Paul Celan

Blackout—in the theater as well as on screen. From a distance we hear Steve Reich's "Music for 18 Musicians." It almost sounds like a train approaching. Now we hear voices: by turns hushed and strident, interrupting each other, impossible to know how many. . . .

Voice: In Czernowitz where I was born
Voice: In Chernovsty where I was born
Voice: In Czernowitz, Bukovina, where I was born
Voice: Even the words Bukovina, Romania
Voice: In Romania where I was born
Voice: Even the words
Voice: Romania, Bukovina.
Voice: Much has been said
Voice: Even the words in the language
Voice: In Czernowitz
Voice: Bukovina Bukovina
Voice: I hear the sounds
Voice: Even the words
Voice: I do not want to describe my memories for you
Voice: Where I was born
Voice: Czernowitz
Voice: Much has been said
Voice: What the land was like
Voice: I do not want to
Voice: Ukrainians of course Romanians Jews
Voice: I hear the sounds
Voice: Where I was born
Voice: Where I was born
Voice: Romanians Jews
Voice: I hear the sounds
Voice: What the land was like
Voice: Even the words
Voice: I hear the sounds

Silence.

Aerial shot rushing over the mountain ranges near Chemovsty: dense pine, spruce and beech trees for miles and miles.

Blinding light.

SCRIPT FOR HOME VIDEO AND FLASHLIGHT

After Federico García Lorca

Black screen for twenty seconds. Suddenly a young girl—say eight or nine years old—turns a flashlight on her face, holding it at the level of her chin.

Young girl:
       When I die
       I'll die in Lancaster, Ohio.
       With the smoke of the glass factory in my hair,
       I'll die in Lancaster, Ohio.

       With my mother's hazel eyes,
       I'll die in Lancaster, Ohio.
       I'll remember blue jays and air guitar
       when I die in Lancaster.
       When I die in Lancaster,
       I'll remember the moon through the 2x4s of my brother's treehouse.
       I'll die in Lancaster.
       I'll die in Lancaster, Ohio,
       with a red bandanna around my neck.
       I'll die in Ohio.
       In a little boat on Rising Park pond,
       in my blue dress with the frayed collar,
       with turkey buzzards circling above me like old grownups,
       I'll die in Lancaster, Ohio.
       I'll die in Lancaster, Ohio,
       with a bag of bread for the ducks.
       I'll die in Lancaster.
       I'll die in Ohio.
       In early evening,
       before fireflies make stars between the trees,
       I'll die in Lancaster, Ohio,
       I swear!

Silence. Smoke comes out of her mouth. Blackout.

IN A HOUSE BESIEGED

1

A colony of ants stripping a mulberry tree of its bark.

Voice-over: "One wants to eat certain words, because they are perfect and embarrassments as well."

2

Black screen.

3

Extreme close-up of tap water dripping from a faucet.

Voice-over: "Both belief and denial throw existence into question."

4

Black screen.

5

A low crashing sound: close-up of an ice-maker dropping cubes into a bucket.

Voice-over: "When I saw that I and my body were not the same, I knew what card to play and played it as soon as my turn came without second-guessing my opponent's position in the game."

6

Black screen.

7

A middle-aged man tearing shingles off a roof, throwing them blindly to the ground.

Voice-over: "Anything named slips out of the mind."

8

Black screen.

9

A young girl hiding in a dark pantry.
    Voice-over: "The shot of a traffic light held too long is no longer a traffic light."

10

Black screen.

11

The girl hugs her knees and rocks back and forth.
    Voice-over: "Refusal more than anything else ends play."

12

Black screen.

13

A FOR SALE sign on the lawn of a suburban house, sun-shot, blinding the camera as it drives by in a car.
    Voice-over: "Can a person who isolates himself do battle with the whole world?"

14

Black screen.

15

A middle-aged woman tripping and falling ungracefully over a dog's chain.
    Voice-over: "One is going to wake and dream and sleep and one is going to wake and dream and sleep."

16

Black screen.

17

Inside the dark pantry. From the girl's point of view the camera moves towards the pantry door, into the door's wood, into the tiniest grain, in which we see

18

the middle-aged woman tripping and falling again ungracefully over a dog's chain;
  Voice-over: "One is going to wake and dream—"

19

the shadow of a cross rushing over a dry lake bed;
  Voice-over: "Childhood doesn't exist."

20

the girl lighting two cigarettes simultaneously, the match-flare lasting impossibly long.
  Voice-over: "Some nighttime kiss I hang over the railing for."

21

Black screen.

22

The girl blinks and rubs her eyes.
  Voice-over: "Dream is another of those perfect and perfectly embarrassing words, pivoting on a misery styled to something greater."

23

Black screen.

24

Trees and shrubs bending in wind.
Voice-over. "We look at our things because they have our respect."

25

Black screen.

26

Twilight. The young girl playing hopscotch on a side-walk. She wears a white sweater that's far too large for her.
Voice-over: "These are stories."

27

Black screen.

28

Close up of the sweater's long sleeves hanging limp past the girl's hands.
Voice-over: "Inside, the ear spins beautiful webs."

29

Black screen.

CINEMA VÉRITÉ: THE COLOR WHEEL

Scene 1. The screen is blue.

Subtitle: Hearings of the House Committee on Un-American Activities, October 30, 1947

Mr. Stripling: Mr. Brecht, will you please state your full name and present address for the record, please? Speak into the microphone.

Mr. Brecht: My name is Bertolt Brecht. I am living at 34 West Seventy-third Street, New York. I was born in Augsburg, Germany, February 10, 1898.

Scene 2. The screen is yellow.

Mr. Stripling: Mr. Brecht, will you please state your full name and present address for the record, please? Speak into the microphone.

Mr. Brecht: My name is Bertolt Brecht. I am living at 34 West Seventy-third Street, New York. I was born in Augsburg, Germany, February 10, 1898.

Scene 3. The screen is red.

Mr. Brecht: My name is Bertolt Brecht. I am living at 34 West Seventy-third Street, New York. I was born in Augsburg, Germany, February 10, 1898.

Scene 5. The screen is green.

Mr. Stripling: Were you ever employed in the motion-picture industry?

Mr. Brecht: Yes, I—yes. I sold a story to a Hollywood firm, "Hangmen Also Die," but I did not write the screenplay myself. I am not a professional screenplay writer.

Scene 6. The screen is brown.

Mr. Stripling: Mr. Brecht, are you a member of the Communist Party or have you ever been a member of the Communist Party?

Mr. Brecht: May I read my statement? I will answer this question but may I read my statement?

Scene 7. The screen is white.

The Chairman: Mr. Brecht, the committee has carefully gone over the statement. It is a very interesting story of German life but it is not at all pertinent to this inquiry. Therefore, we do not care to have you read the statement.

Scene 8. The screen is purple.

Mr. Stripling: Mr. Brecht, did you ever make application to join the Communist Party?

Mr. Brecht: No, no, no, no, no, never.

Scene 9. The screen is black.

Mr. Brecht: No, no, no, no, no, never.

Scene 10. The screen is white.

Mr. Brecht: No, no, no, no, no, never.

The Temptation of Saint Augustine

ARGUMENT

One of the most moving passages in *The Confessions* is the one in which Augustine recounts sending his concubine, the woman he lived with for fifteen years and the mother of his only child, away from him and their son:

> The woman with whom I shared my bed was torn from my side. . . . My heart still clung to her: it was pierced and wounded within me. . . . She returned to Africa, vowing that she would never know another man, and leaving with me our natural son.

His concubine was torn away, Augustine says, not out of religious scrupulosity. In a fit of worldly ambition he decided to follow his mother Monica's advice and to marry a wealthy heiress. Monica desperately wanted her son to convert to Catholicism; lacking that, he should at least respect his position as Rhetorician to the Imperial Court in Milan, one of the choice academic jobs to be had at the time, and find a partner worthy of his status and prestige. She had, in fact, found him such a partner, the ten-year-old daughter of a wealthy Milanese gentleman, and arranged the marriage. Augustine would be rich for the rest of his life. He agreed to the arrangement. At age 32, his future was set.

But something happened. Augustine decided not to marry. He resigned from his imperial position. The shock of loss he experienced, his regret over having dismissed summarily the woman he loved, urged him to confront his growing love of Christ and to begin his ascetic life in earnest, something he'd been contemplating for years. That, at any rate, is how I read his decision to relinquish "all earthly desire, no longer seeking wife, children of the flesh, riches or worldly honors," as his former student Possidius put it in the first biography of Augustine, *Sancti Augustini Vita* (432 A.D.).

Adeodatus, the child, stayed with his father in Milan. He was fourteen years old. Augustine acknowledges candidly in *The Confessions* that Adeodatus was unwanted, but the experience of fatherhood was transformative. He deeply loved Adeodatus, who proved to be very much his father's son: intellectually brilliant, an earnest seeker of truth with a capital T.

Adeodatus entered the Catholic Church on the same day as his father, in the same baptism ceremony. His death at age seventeen must have been devastating for both parents (though perhaps Adeodatus's mother never learned of his death; Augustine never mentions telling her).

Augustine's baptism marked the end of, or at least the final sea-change in, his lifelong struggle with a triad of conflicting desires: the desire for a loving and sexual domestic life, the longing for a severe life devoted to God, and his fierce need for worldly success. Still, it's hard to imagine a man as dutiful and as quivering with sensitivity as Augustine not being haunted by the memory of his concubine. When he dismissed her his heart was "pierced and wounded"; she had to be "torn" from him. Who was she? What tempest did she and Augustine endure as a result of being together?

This work borrows its structure from an early Christian art form: the triptych. Used primarily as altarpieces, triptychs consisted of three separate but interpenetrating panels placed side by side, thus honoring and emulating the mystery of the Holy Trinity.

While triptychs were originally organized around images of Christ and the Virgin, eventually saints were also treated as their central subjects. As a scholar of triptychs, Shirley Neilson Blum, puts it, "As saints began to be placed in the center of triptychs, they were not depicted as isolated cult images. Indeed they were shown more dramatically in scenes from their lives."

Placing Saint Augustine and his concubine (and what a forbearing and bewildered saint she must have been) in the center of a triptych seemed appropriate for the same reason: to show them dramatically, in scenes from their lives.

Lord, give me chastity and abstinence, but not yet.
—Saint Augustine, *The Confessions*

Left Panel

Throughout the year 385 A.D.

. . . chastity and abstinence,
but not yet.

Bronze bees, blue hawks, ochre horses.

Not yet.

Bells ring, deepening the fog.

Not yet.

White oxen, slabs of salt, Egyptian cotton.

Not yet.

A serving dish with guinea-fowls.

Not yet.

A basket of speckled pears, blue figs, green grapes.

Not yet.

Her face engulfed by shadow: cobalt blue, then red.

Blinding light.

The bridge of his nose.

Blinding light.

Her right eyebrow.

Blinding light.

In shadow, then out of shadow, his face: cobalt blue.

Listen to me.

Her chin seen from the floor.

Listen to me.

His knees seen from the ceiling.

A pool with shade trees, lily pads, goldfish, drooping willows.

His face in shadow: blue orange, red.

Sitting, her knees touching his as they argue.

Cobalt blue.

Children poking sticks into the entrails of a dead snake.

Hush.

You block my view to God.

Adeodatus just ate. Hungry?

Listen to me.

Your eyes are hazel flecked with green.

Rain. Rain.

Olive leaves: dark green on top, light green on bottom.

Blue hawks in strong sunlight.

Children poking sticks.

I've been thinking of you.

His blunt thumb parting her labia.

Full moon in a rattan dish.

Listen.

I have no reason to lie to you.

Winter's almost here.

Bells ring.

Sharp memory: throwing Adeodatus into the air high as a kite!

Deepening the fog.

Whispering into the tiny ear: *Adeodatus*.

You block my view.

A basket of speckled pears, blue figs, green grapes.

It's because of me you're wasting your afternoon?

Rain.

Hush.

Her left hand rousing his glans.

I promise not to make fun of you anymore.

Stay with me.

Listen.

Blinding light.

You disgust me.

Listen.

I love you.

Green grapes.

Cobalt blue.

Mimosa, tiger and canna lilies.

You block my view to God.

Cobalt blue.

Moonlight concentrates on the empty piazza.

Lilacs, orchids, daffodils.

Beside you I feel nothing but longing.

Full moon.

You taught me the sweetness of an hour.

Stop all this talking!

Horses on the road whinnying.

You're like a large, unmade bed.

People are starving and you're worried about a kiss!

It's no sin to talk to people.

The city's thick walls of granite.

To burn with desire and keep quiet about it.

Blur. Blur.

Children poking sticks.

I want you to look at me.

What's happened is that you're no longer a real woman.

Stiff breezes and Adeodatus shivering.

You're not of good blood.

I love you.

You know nothing about women.

Blur.

Quarter moon.

I'm not thinking about anything.

Fat warblers rolled in spiced egg yolk.

You *want* God to punish you!

Blue onslaught of wind.

God is God.

Thistledown.

Thin slices of bread brushed with olive oil.

The whole town's talking about you.

A convulsive rippling through his body.

Long bars of red sunlight.

You make me want to spit.

Dormice rolled in thyme-flavored honey and poppy seeds.

Dusk in the city square.

Blue hawks.

Keep away from me.

Don't scream.

Overripe pumpkins.

Faint starlight.

Night-flowering jasmine vines.

Throwing Adeodatus into the air.

It's no sin.

One slice of bread covered with milled chicken liver mixed with sage and anchovy.

You block my view.

Stubborn pulse against the throat.

Open-mouthed kisses.

Pray for me.

Texture of muscle, bone, flesh.

Whispering into the tiny ear: *Adeodatus.*

Every soul has a lower part directed towards the bodily and a higher part directed towards the intelligible.

Her legs perched on his back.

Rose, blackberry, iris.

Let me wash your hair.

The sweetness of an hour.

Glittering arc of your back.

Leaves take light in sympathy and greed.

You in your round straw hat and nothing else!

Bright looming dark.

Butterflies, shearmice, bats.

Remember when you lifted my dress in the dark arbor?

Grape-hull barley cakes.

Crisp kisses, then her legs straddling his neck.

Bronze bees.

Forgive me, Christ, a thief from another tree.

He blushes, turning purple.

Olive leaves: dark green on top.

Strict pleasure of affection.

Swallows darting in early light.

The boy's fierce, cautious body.

Blinding light.

Your wet hair weighs ten pounds!

Radish stems with garlic for breakfast.

Honeybrown skin on your back.

Adeodatus's pudgy hands getting into everything at the market.

The finch's yellow is stronger than the sun's.

Listen to me.

Saddlebags on a copper-colored donkey.

It is necessary to have a body to feel bodily chastisement.

A young man leaning on a hoe.

By the road: nettles, thistle, barley, crickets, horses, wayfarers.

Her left hand lightly drawing his penis to size.

Hush.

The soul is invisible and the body is visible.

His artless thumb parting her labia.

A basket of blue cornflowers.

The soul is in the body as the skill is in the instrument.

Herbs cooked in wine, bread dipped in wine.

O fountain of mercies!

Her left hand rousing his glans.

Adeodatus batting the air with his fists.

The harp of her ribcage.

Cobalt blue.

Kissing the prolonged slope under her chin.

Beyond the beauty of morning or evening star.

Her hand gripping his arm.

Milan is sodden with fog and wet snow.

The flat of his tongue warm against her sex.

Morning or evening star.

Blur. Blur.

Lacerating abandon.

Stubborn pulse.

Hush.

Her arched back, her tense buttocks.

The soul is outside the body of the world.

Her otherness crushes him.

The filth of my body, wash away.

Your foreskin looks parched, hurtful.

The defilements of my soul, wash away.

Dense fog, then three-foot snow drifts.

Aggressive sudden suction of her mouth.

Texture of muscle, bone, flesh.

Dusk. The smell of honeysuckle.

Gyre of navel and shadowy black pubic triangle.

Her fishlike nibbles on his broad shoulder blades.

Incessant throbbing underneath her.

Apricots, grated walnuts.

Listen to me.

Half-flooded roads in Milan.

Sweet, slick thrusts.

Whirling snow.

Throwing Adeodatus into the air.

Her lapis earrings.

Figs drowned in honey.

You have body after body.

Holly trees catching snowflakes.

Knees raised, legs open, hips tilted, mouth a riot of grunts and whistles.

She makes a snowball and hurls it at him, laughing.

A convulsive rippling through his body.

Dusk. Atop an archway, a preening stork.

Belly. Belly.

More tongue-tied than grass.

Her eyelids fluttering closed.

Body after body.

His mouth plunging onto her breast.

The air smells like snow.

Thighs spreading.

Nipples erected above puckered aureolas.

Cataract of bliss.

The taut glimmer of her oval thigh.

Her lips a frank O.

Hush.

His galvanizing little jumps.

Cobalt blue.

More tongue-tied than grass.

Her strong hands messaging his deltoids, pectorals, the back of his neck.

Listen to me.

I go from loving you to total despair to loving God to total despair again in
the space of half an hour.

Fish-naked, they drink date wine in little cups.

Let me wash your hair.

The dull raspberry color of your sex.

Starlight.

What is purification but the separation of the soul from the body?

Wild pig with garlic and mustard.

Body after body.

She strums a harp made of tortoise-shell and boxwood.

Sheep huddle, their backs to the wind.

Broth and plovers' eggs.

Sweet Christ, have mercy on my oddness!

Leeks, parsley, shallots.

Adeodatus, a young man, shivering.

Under his vermilion-stained wool cap, he sweats like a horse.

You're daft with wine!

190

Soldiers sleep under piles of blankets outside a bathhouse.

His face: blue, orange, blue.

Speech is a long, twisting lane.

Artichoke butter.

A mouse scurries into a pile of straw.

In that boy I had nothing but the sin.

Impossible to leave you.

Whispering into the tiny ear.

I'm leaving you.

Delusion came because I wanted it.

Certain words will not fade from memory.

You're forever looking at the river girls!

She stands on tiptoe when they hug.

Long, twisting lane.

I'm leaving you.

Pearls and spices from Carthage.

Soft, soft flesh.

There's the woodpecker that carries your soul when you're asleep.

Her feet hooked around his thighs.

The body's eye does not see.

The sting of grinding.

In my wretchedness.

Sucking her slender fingers.

Fish-naked.

Sweet Christ.

Generous, merciless word.

Adeodatus shivering.

That I may take food as I take medicine.

Credo quin absurdum.

Her tongue inside his lower lip.

Unimaginable word.

Veal with seven lemon halves.

The bed smells of cinnamon.

Puckered aureolas.

Restorative word.

Beads of semen like aloe drops across her hip.

More tongue-tied than grass.

You look like you've swallowed a torchlight!

Yellow, red, green peppers roasted on rare shrimp, clams, mussels, more cut
    lemons.

As I take medicine.

Look me in the eye and tell me this isn't Monica's handiwork.

Crystalline word.

Sliced eggs and rue on bread.

Shattering word.

Goose liver, zucchini, raw artichoke, wild asparagus.

Mercy on my oddness.

Slick birdlime of pleasure.

Look at me.

Quickening word.

Listen

Infinite word.

to me remember

Word inside the

me remember my stiff

generous word merciless

satyr blushing purple listen

enormous word enormous

to me hush listen

worship delirious

to me.

worship.

Central Panel

370—385 A.D.

Her name is a breath withheld for centuries. In his ninety-three books, in the four hundred sermons and three hundred letters that have survived, Saint Augustine did not once utter her name.

She shared his bed for fifteen years. She followed him from Thagaste to Carthage to Thagaste again to Carthage again to Rome to Milan. She bore him a son, whom he reluctantly agreed to call Adeodatus ('given by God').

They were one flesh.

But she inhabits no word.

Saint Augustine finished *The Confessions* in 400 A.D. Unlike Saint Thomas Aquinas, who upon abandoning the *Summa Theologica* declared that *All I have written is as so much straw compared to what I have seen and what has been revealed to me*, Saint Augustine had a more idiosyncratic and human response upon finishing his great book of memory:

—I have made a gift to God of all my memories, he said to his friend Alypius. Except one. One I have kept for myself.

They met when he was sixteen, a timid student of law and rhetoric who longed to be a bad boy, though he did not have the stomach for it. To his disgrace, he was courteous to his elders and respectful of his teachers. Worse still, he loved poetry. He even wept over it.

He was all awkward leanness. With her he pretended to be full of himself, but she saw through this. He stammered while trying to boast of a prodigious act of memory or of an eloquent essay he had written at school. She laughed affectionately.

She looked to be the same age as Augustine; she did not know for sure. Her tawny intelligent face sang to him, even the freckles across her forehead and nose, even her sweating upper lip. She was not shy but calm, kind. Her kindness eclipsed his, he thought. (He was forever comparing himself to her and finding himself lacking, which in turn made her feel continually judged.) Unlike his own clumsy, intermittent struggle to be generous to the things of this world, she seemed *effortlessly* kind—to strangers, animals, damaged trees and plants as easily as to her own family. He could not get his mind around it.

She was a devout Catholic. This he could not countenance. For as long as he knew her, he tried to argue her out of the embarrassment of Catholicism.

She worshipped in the same church in Thagaste, a basilica that resembled a barn, as his mother, Monica. Monica would see her during Mass: a bony teenager wrapped in faded blue linen who kept her head bowed a second or two longer than most after praying.

Monica thought the child was putting on airs: a girl from a family of freed slaves acting as pious as she herself!

But Augustine, who avoided going to church if at all possible, noticed the pretty young woman too, and started attending more regularly.

On their first outing together he lost a handsome spoon.

He had taken her to the manicured wilderness of his patron's estate. Romanian had told him to use the grounds and the library as he saw fit. He saw fit to take his attractive companion to the grounds—out of the sight of Monica—as often as she was willing.

They walked through a dwarf orchard of pear and apple trees. A light breeze stirred the speckled leaves. Butterflies spiraled across the cut grass. He asked if she would sit with him within a half-circle of arborvitae.

She nodded hazily, taking in the splendor.

He began unpacking the basket of fruit (quince, pomegranate, plum, pear) he'd brought along to impress her. At once, with an audible gasp, he discovered that a spoon was missing. It was a small intricate silver spoon, an heirloom of Monica's, who would sorely miss it. Had his companion seen it fall from the basket? No, she had not.

After what seemed to her only a cursory, directionless search, he suggested they consult a diviner named Albicerius.

—I wouldn't plant a bulb before consulting Albicerius, said Augustine, trying to hide his seizure of panic.

Is he joking? she wondered. She wasn't sure, so she stifled the impulse to laugh.

They walked in silence from Romanian's estate to the center of town. He stooped as he walked, as if at any second he would turn over a stone to look for insects. She followed wordlessly, appreciating the gravity of the moment.

In a dingy alley in Thagaste, in a tiny room whose foul odor—a mixture of sweet perfume and sour human sweat—they smelled ten paces before entering, they found Albicerius. She covered her mouth and nose.

The chamber was unbearably warm. Albicerius—giant, sagging—sat fanning himself before a rickety table made of laurel branches. On the table was a bronze bowl, inside which were inscribed the letters of the alphabet. Over the bowl, hung from a wooden frame by a piece of string, a gold ring swung freely. Albicerius set the ring swinging to and fro over the letters of the alphabet, spelling out message after message from the great beyond.

Does he really buy into this. . . this hokum? she kept wondering.

—I can tell you where your spoon is all right, Albicerius said. But why settle for that, Aurelius? I will tell you every—

—No, no, no! said Augustine, holding the palms of his hands over his ears. Just tell me about the spoon!

Her laughter was loud, unmalicious, endless.

Eye-stinging noon.

They sat on a rocky crag overlooking Romanian's olive groves and vinerows. In the air was a keen sweet smell of wild oregano. Occasionally a bottom-heavy cloud passed over them.

He read Virgil to her, *The Aeneid*, Book IV. She recognized the shapely cadences of formal Latin from the priests at the basilica. But Augustine added something different to those cadences: an urgency, a kind of fury combined with cool precision. She did not understand each word but she gauged each word's weight and pitch. The rhythms entered her. It was like dancing to a grave, God-haunted music.

He paused briefly to explain the story. Dido was about to kill herself after being abandoned by Aeneas, who had left her at Jupiter's command.

At least, let me die. Thus, thus! I go to the dark, go gladly. . . .
She had spoken; and with these words, her attendants saw her falling
Upon the sword, they could see the blood spouting up over
The blade, and her hands spattered. Their screams rang to the roofs of
The palace; then rumour ran amok through the shocked city.
All was weeping and wailing, the streets were filled with a keening
Of women, the air resounded with terrible lamentations.
It was as if Carthage or ancient Tyre should be falling,
With enemy troops breaking into the town and a conflagration
Furiously sweeping over the abodes of men and of gods.

He had to stop reading and wipe his tears.

—I'm sorry, he said. This is embarrassing.

—No, no, she said. Not at all.

The intensity of his feeling endeared him to her. She had never seen a man weep over a woman's fate, let alone a woman who existed only in Latin words. A man who shed tears for Dido could be trusted to treat a woman well, to not abandon her.

They explored Romanian's estate every day for a week. Then they began meeting there at night.

She loved the uncut meadows beyond the black cypresses, the sky bruise-blue and scattered with stars.

If they could arrange to meet at dusk, she loved noting the exact moment when twilight extinguished itself into night and watching the moon climb the trellis of dark. Then she could imagine beyond Romanian's tall meadows the miles and miles of deeper dark all the way to the sea.

He talked theatrically of crossing that sea, the thought of which secretly terrified him.

But what really interested him was her hidden body, the promise of its voluptuous grip.

Without his knowing it, she taught him how to kiss her, their joined mouths adjusting, testing. Abruptly he gathered up the courage to put a hand in her lap. She started to laugh, it was such an artless, awkward gesture. But she took his hand and frankly guided two of his fingers into her; he touched speculatively her petaled interior.

She stood and disrobed. He stared in wonder at the shadowy triangle between her legs. Amid the fur he could distinguish flat circlets of dark hair. Catullus had compared a woman's sexual hair to fern leaves. Accurate enough, he thought; but Catullus had said nothing about the dark circlets.

Her naked body was pale brown. The sharp angles implied by her bony arms were softened with a kind of flesh he'd seen only briefly before: supple, substantial, *womanly*, he thought.

Staring: gyre of navel, puckered aureole.

He touched her clavicle, her breasts, the cleft between her breasts. There was a pleasant glint in her eyes. His throat made a rasping sound.

She indicated that he should remove his belt and tunic.

He disrobed and was embarrassed. Consciousness afflicted him. His arms were sticklike. His thin chest lacked manly heft. The horns of his pelvis stuck out. No doubt his penis was too slender and short. He decided at that moment to grow a beard.

Poor tortured boy, she thought, he's going to need some help.

O thrusting inside the soft moist secret flesh!
     This much he knew:
     God is a poor substitute for the stances of love.

Augustine's father, Patricius, was moody, hoarse from collecting taxes and yelling at his chickens, and mostly invisible. He knew he was no match for Monica, and wandered from mistress to mistress. What remaining time he had he spent in the town forum among friends, drinking, boasting, gossiping. He kept out of Monica's life as much as possible. She, however, did not return the favor. She lectured him nightly on his moral leprosy (a phrase she used the way others used a cattle prod)—the poor example he set by not becoming a Christian. Remarkably, his mistresses were never brought up as part of his greater failing, for which he was grateful.

Augustine blamed his father for sharpening Monica's narrowness of mind to a fine point. For that Augustine could never forgive him. His mother's daily, interminable barrage against the evils of sex was, he knew, a case of the sins of the father visited upon the son. The son did not care to be so visited.

The small plot of land Patricius farmed was sour. Out of it he was able to eke some corn and olives for his family, but none to profit from. At least his chickens were dutifully reproductive.

Still, Patricius was a proud man. As the oldest son, this will all be yours some day, he said to Augustine with a sweeping gesture.

No thanks, Augustine wanted to sneer, but instead he said thoughtfully:

—There's no need to think about that for a long time, Father.

Patricius smiled, and wrung the neck of a dazed chicken.

Augustine determined to rid himself of his father's baleful energies. A year ago at the baths Patricius noticed that Augustine had reached puberty. Pointing and laughing proudly, gathering the other fathers around him, he said, That's my boy! That's my boy! and slapped Augustine several times on the back.

Augustine shivered in disgust. He did not want to be Patricius's son. The marks of puberty embarrassed him. Did their fruition mean he would be as cruel to women as Patricius was to Monica? Did they insure that he could not be satisfied with one woman? Perhaps it would better to forego sex altogether. Yes. That was the best option. Thinking of his mother's sufferings, that day he resolved never to explore the bitter dominion of sex. Instead he would pursue what truly mattered: words, those precious cups of meaning.

The gift of wise words and the courage to live them.

Monica and Patricius split their sons, Solomon-like. Augustine was hers. She decided that Augustine was too brilliant, his future too vital, to allow him to spend much time with her husband. She would give her husband Navigius, the younger son. Navigius was simple like his father, utterly lacking his brother's quickness of mind and complex understanding. He studied doggedly without effect before leaving school to join his father on his tax-collecting rounds and on the farm and at the forum. To Patricius's delight, Navigius grew into a thick, surly, loud-mouthed image of his father.

Perpetua, the youngest, remained at home, helping Monica assign housekeeping chores to the slaves and keeping her company on daily trips to the ovens and the market. She thus freed Augustine to fling himself into every nook and cranny of Thagaste. Perpetua aspired to her mother's piety and indifference to men. She too was small and shiny, like a pear lit up brightly from within.

The concubine's family lived surprisingly well. A freed slave, her father now made a decent wage as a salt vendor. He was expected to pay daily homage to the family of his former master, who on his deathbed freed all his slaves, and was happy to do so. As a young man he had spent four numbing years at the marble quarries in Chemtou, where he was converted to Christianity by a fellow slave. The disparity between his former and present lives made him stammer with gratitude.

Her mother taught her the art of dressmaking. Together they made a formidable team, weaving a variety of tunic styles: the loose-knit, the close-knit, the linen-blue, the interior, the goldedge, the marigold, the mantilla, the royal, the wavy, the waxy. Their tunics were sought out especially for the brilliance of their colors: dark and pale rose, amethyst, sea-green, scarlet, myrtle, saffron—the dyes alchemized skillfully from shellfish and vegetables.

Her industry, her handsome self-sufficiency, both attracted and intimidated Augustine.

The sharp outline of her freckled cheekbone. The black tousled hair. The widening hips. The harp of her ribcage. The lovely, maddening glimmer of her bared breasts.

The quince trees, the cypresses, the swallowing dark down to the sea were all wasted on him.

Was he a moral leper, as his mother insisted? He knew that, given a chance, desire overcame scruple. He knew he was giving it that chance. But there was a kind of secret ripeness in him. He had not known about that. What was it for?

He could not get his mind around it.

I promise not to laugh, she said.

     Wind fingered her hair. Maple leaves fidgeted on their branches.

     —But you *will* laugh, he said.

     —I won't. I promise. Read the poem.

     —OK. But it's not finished.

     He cleared his throat.

> I want to be
> The ivory pin
> In your wild hair.

     —That's it? she said. I mean, you wrote that for me?

     —Who else? he said.

     —Nobody has ever, *ever*, written a poem for me.

     —So you like it? he said. You think it's a good poem? I was going to say '*carved* ivory pin' but I wasn't sure. What do you think? You can be brutal with me.

     She was silent for some time. Then she said:

     —I don't want to be brutal with you.

Leaves took light in sympathy and greed.

There was a discipline to attention. Love was teaching it to him.

That eucalyptus tree by the bend in the road, dusty, sun-stunned, was not just a eucalyptus tree.

How he loved to talk!

During a single hurried breakfast he could exhaust any number of topics without seeming to pause for breath: African sunlight ('the Queen of all color'), the lame plays of Plautus and Terence, the virtues of sweeping, his father's newest mistress, digestion as a source of misery, flies, forelegs, his mother's sanctity, the presence of evil in owls, eyes, the stupid opening acts at the circus, whether God was eminent or imminent, poisonous vs. nonpoisonous snakes, his unthinkably bad and unruly students, the lack of shade in Thagaste, the tedium of well-traveled Romans, the sea as compared to a glass of water, the smell of night-flowering jasmine vines, Socrates' forbearance, Alypius's chastity.

—What do you think? he'd occasionally ask her.

But before she had a chance to respond he was off and running again, pursuing God only knows what honeycombs of thought.

Monica had a gift for dreaming. Needful or heartsick, she consulted her dreams the way Augustine consulted Albecirius. The dreams, like all gifts, came from God, who spoke in them with such force and ease and intimacy and consolation that she never wanted to wake. Once wakened, though, she experienced an enveloping calm that lasted for days—or until Augustine's rough habits wore her down and inclined her exhausted mind to dread.

One morning she announced brightly that the previous night's dream had assured her he would become a baptized Catholic, and during her lifetime.

—My prayers will be answered, she said with a confidence that annoyed him.

He decided to annoy her in turn. He said:

—Do I have a say in what I am to become? Or does God not care about free will?

He hated sounding like a smartass student; he hated her for provoking him to sound like one. Though he would never admit it to her, he envied Monica her dreams. Upon hearing of the way God visited her in her sleep, he thought: I might as well read Cicero all night, my dreams are so boring.

Dido made an effort to raise her heavy eyes,
Then gave it up: the sword-blade grated against her breast bone.
Three times she struggled to rise, to lift herself on an elbow,
Three times rolled back on the bed. Her wandering gaze went up
To the sky, looking for light: she gave a moan when she saw it.

That day they read no further.

In the mornings he needed to give a shape to the previous night's ecstasies and humiliations by disclosing them to Alypius. He could not let them go unremarked upon. That would leave them leached of meaning. Keeping the nights to himself (as he assumed she did), allowing the subterranean murmur of inner dialogue to be his only council, was impossible.

Alypius, listening to yet another morning-after narrative, worried about his lovestruck friend. So did Augustine's other friends. They arranged to gather at the forum one afternoon after a lecture and confront Augustine, an interrogation board of four sixteen-year-olds in pretentious white togas.

Alypius began the inquisition. His voice, breaking, croaked out:

—We're worried about you, my friend. You're not yourself these days. This woman—fuck her, put your hands into her as into a loaf of bread. But for God's sake don't fall in love with her!

Evodius was the prissy, stagy one. He said:

—She has no fleshy charms. Her breasts are plums. Fine when you want a plum, but not when you want a gourd.

—What can you possibly talk to her about? asked Nebridius. 'Nice weather we're having, don't you agree?'

—'How is your soup, my love?' added Licentius, snickering.

—I know, Evodius said. She's secretly a formidable philosopher, and she argues with you about Aristotle's *Categories* until the wee hours.

The interrogation board cackled and hooted at that one.

Augustine tried unsuccessfully to come up with one witty response after another. He gave up trying.

—I don't know what to say, he said at last. You're not wrong to question me. I don't understand it myself.

Then, placing his hands on his knees as if to brace himself against the windblast of their derision, he added:

—I'm moving to Carthage, and I'm taking her with me.

It had not occurred to him to take her anywhere until he uttered the words.

The interrogation board sat in stunned silence, looking at their sandals.

After seeing him each day and most nights for two months, she assessed this odd, tense sixteen-year-old. In addition to his sympathy for Dido, he had five things going for him.

He was not decrepit.

He was not betrothed.

His awkwardness implied an inner life.

He was not perpetually drunk.

He was not *entirely* inept at love.

In these ways he distinguished himself from the other men she knew.

He had, however, a large mark against him. He was not a Catholic.

He was, in fact, contemptuous of Catholics—so much so that her mother and father forbade her to see him after he let slip in their presence a joke about Pope Damasus's popularity among the female population in Rome.

—Idiot! she felt duty-bound to say in front of her scandalized parents. How can you say such a thing? You know we worship Christ and obey the Pope.

—He apologized at once, claiming exhaustion and a distracted mind after too many hours reading books. But her father had heard more than enough from this rude heathen, and banished him from the house.

Later that night, after she sneaked out to make love with him at Romanian's estate, the clover and peppergrass mussing her hair, he said to her, shockingly:

—What harm can come from joking about a *Catholic*? If it helps your parents see the light, so much the better.

The next morning, her aloofness confirmed his suspicion that he had gone too far. His friends, he knew, would congratulate him for having stood up for the Truth (they would also be pleased that he had allowed himself to contradict her), but he decided not report this episode to them. Her aloofness felt murderous. He needed to make amends. Her aloofness was a challenge, an insinuation of his failure. He needed her to feel close to him again.

—I don't know what came over me, he said to her. My mind fastens on a thing and turns it over and over like a piece of glass. And then I cut myself on it. And then other people get cut too.

—You're normally so sweet, she said. It's as if you became a different person.

—I'll be a *better* person, I promise. To prove it, I want you to come with me to Carthage. Romanian has guaranteed my tuition. I'll be able to finish my studies.

—You want me to go with you to Carthage? That's what you really want?

—Yes.

Saying it, he believed it.

That night she had a vision of the future.

It was of his receding backside.

Still, she knew at once that she would accept his invitation. She would break her parents' hearts. Salvation, which once beckoned daily, would lie far away, invisible as grief, mute as granite. She would go to Carthage.

And all because of some ill-defined promise in his scraggly face.

And because he would someday take her across the sea beyond Romanian's uncut meadows.

And because she was pregnant.

It's out of the question, he said. I can't have a child. Albicerius gave me the name of a woman who'll sell us an abortifacient. The price is not cheap but it's worth twice whatever she wants.

She looked at him as though he were a tree stump.

How could she have aligned herself with a man who would suggest aborting a vivid emissary from God—the ministering presence of a new life? She unleashed on him an outraged rectitude that seemed to her merely obvious:

—This child will come into the world with your blessing and your love. He is a *gift*. Don't you know that? God has spoken to us in the most direct terms.

He let out a petulant snarl. Pink anger suffused his cheeks. His forehead appeared to enlarge. She was undaunted.

Eventually he calmed down enough to mumble a question:

—'He'? You said 'he'?

—All the signs, she said, tell me it's going to be a boy. His name is Adeodatus.

Augustine, stunned that his illiterate mistress had followed Berber custom and come up with the Latin for 'given by God,' simply sighed before burying his head in his hands.

Walking to Romanian's estate the next afternoon in the pitiless heat, he couldn't believe his fate. He was moving to Carthage, the Rome of Africa, the Empire's most treacherous and salacious and exciting city, *hampered by a pregnant woman*. A child was going to call him *father*.

He walked past Romanian's gate and into the unmanicured acres of scrub, thornbush, thickets of weeds. Before him, the screes of a steep mountain, and stone outcrops drenched in the lichen sunlight.

Father.

The crickets were shriller than he'd ever heard.

Alypius stopped by Augustine's house on the way to a lecture. Listen, Alypius said, I'm sorry about the ambush the other day.

—Ambush? Augustine said.

—You know, when we ganged up on you about your, your concubine.

—Oh, that.

—We were all, especially Evodius, insulting and raunchy. I regret it. All the same, I don't understand what you're doing. I've known women. I've had sex. Sex is nothing. It's more fun to watch chariot races than to ejaculate into a woman's vagina. You've read Marcus Aurelius—

—Of course, Augustine said. 'A release of slime by rubbing a woman's innards.' That's his most generous description of sex.

—Well, Alypius said, he's right!

Augustine laughed. You're lucky to feel that way, he said. You have no idea how lucky you are to feel that way.

I *am* a moral leper, he thought. I've assaulted this prone, stolid creature with my confused lust and impregnated her with a solid acre of darkness.

My exertions are lewd and brutal. When I'm finished, I look at her damp dark hair and semen-stained *palla** and wonder how she could possibly lead me to such stammering fanfares of joy.

He began worshipping with the Manichees as soon as he arrived in Carthage, and wept during hymns in praise of virginity.

*Hood on a tunic

I have tasted a sweet taste. I found nothing sweeter
than the word of Truth. Taste.
I tasted a sweet taste. I found nothing sweeter
than the taste of God. Taste.
I tasted a sweet taste. I found nothing sweeter
than Christ. Wisdom invites you, that you may eat
with your Spirit.

En route to Carthage, after traveling through a forest of cork trees and laurel bushes, they stopped for the night in Bulla Regia. Arranging for their room in one of the city's cool underground houses, Augustine and his companion saw a woman with an iron collar welded to her neck. They walked closer to the woman and, when they were sure she was not looking, read the collar's thickly-lettered inscription: *ADULTERA MERETRIX: TENE ME QVIA FVGAVI A BVLLA REGIA* ('Adulterous prostitute: hold me, because I have run away from Bulla Regia').

Later, as they lay in bed, Augustine said:

—Why is the collar necessary? I mean, in this terrain, if she escaped, where could she possibly run away to?

The concubine yawned, and said:

—She'd run to her family. But her family wouldn't want her. So she'd keep running. And then no one would ever be able to find her.

Her eyes closed into sleep, but not before she added:

—Ever ever ever.

They could smell Carthage before they could see it. The sharp odor of brine and sea air wafted over Byrsa Hill, the last rise blocking a view of the city. Cresting the hill they found themselves entering an immense stone forum overlooking the town founded by his beloved Dido and, beyond it, the distant glitter of the sea.

He took in the wide grid below: blocks of streets, walls, houses, public buildings interrupted by large shapes he recognized as a theater, an amphitheater, the snaking line of an aqueduct, a cistern, baths. Bees in a brimming hive, Virgil had written of Carthaginians. Just so, Augustine thought.

Looking to the southern edge of the city, to the water's edge, he saw two adjacent harbors. One was circular, with a circular island in its center: a blue-green iris surrounding a stone pupil. The other harbor was rectangular and bustling, dotted with hundreds of undulating twigs that were in fact merchant and war ships.

Descending the hill into the city, he was drawn, hypnotized, to the water. For years he had heard of the sea's sheer immensity but nothing had prepared him for its lulling, erotic *sound*: thrusting, withdrawing, raking the sand, sighing, hissing.

She too was dazzled and delighted but not hypnotized. Her father had been to the sea. He told her it sounded like the wind at Chemtou, wind shredding cypress branches before a thunderstorm. He had told her it held a mirror to the sky, and undressed twice a day.

Augustine couldn't decide what it was like. He stood staring, his mouth open.

The sea was a peacock looking at its own spread tail.
    No.
    The sea was an aloe leaf trembling in somebody's palm.
    Maybe.

The tiny round body stirred in Augustine unknown depths. He learned the child's storms, its quiverings—what nettled it, what calmed it. His offkey humming, he discovered with amazement, made Adeodatus grin like a floating angel. The boy knew his father. The father dilated with joy.

Augustine's concubine attended and provided, soothed and ogled, with continual impossible grace. She was harassed throughout the long nights, especially when tips of new teeth sprouted in Adeodatus's gums, but seemed to float, too, offering her painful breasts and preparing syrups and bean paste without appearing to need any rest at all.

During the days the room was sunlit and airy, freshened by hyacinth and rosemary from a nearby garden. He loved to toss Adeodatus into the air, whispering *Up Adeodatus, down Adeodatus!*, the child squealing with wide delight.

You awake?

Stillness of midnight. Starlight drifting into the mud-brick room.

—*Hush*. You'll wake him.

—I've been thinking.

—Oh no.

—Why does any—

—I'm telling you. Don't even start.

—Why does anything exist? I mean, why does the world exist, and not nothing?

Her patience snapped.

—You! You'd find something to worry about even if there *were* nothing!

The baby, startled awake, dumped on their heads its heavy cry.

Put in me a holy heart, my God: let an upright Spirit be new within me.

The holy heart is Christ: if He rises in us, we also shall rise in Him.

Christ has risen, the dead shall rise with Him. If we believe in Him, we shall pass beyond death and come to life.

The hinge of his swarthy wrist would not cooperate.

It wasn't pliant enough. He couldn't rotate, jiggle, circle, smooth, caress, trace and retrace her enflamed sex the way it cried out to be. Her hips moved her vulva into his fingers, her corneas shone before her eyelids fluttered shut, he brought her to a sudden precipice. Then, as though it had a life of its own, his aching wrist lost its rhythm and couldn't find it again. He gave up.

—I shouldn't have let myself come in your mouth, he said. I'd be of use to you now.

He pouted, humiliated. She understood. She wet a cloth and placed it on his fevered brow. He wanted to lash out at her, but her tenderness, her perfect, unoppressive tenderness. . . .

What *now*?

    —Does evil happen because we will it, or because we ourselves are evil?

    —Aren't you tired yet?

    —If we will it, then before willing it we are innocent.

    —Let *me* sleep at least.

    —If we ourselves—

    —Shhh. You'll wake Adeodatus.

    —are evil then we can't do otherwise than sin. It's out—

    —*Hush*, for heaven's sakes!

    —of our hands, so to speak. In which case—

    —!

Withdrawing from her body after making love, their sweats drying, his guilt patrolled the ochre room. Already he was gone, banished to some doomed place in his punishing mind. Sometimes he had fits, shaking, more tongue-tied than grass. He felt utterly separated from her, from all human beings, their bothersome needs and ridiculous perceptions. He was absent, too, from himself: Aurelius, a vacancy with a name.

He looked like a cornered fox.

She listened to his body, her hand skimming the flesh on his back, patiently coaxing his return. She called on Christ to help him.

She urged him to look through their window to the northern fields tilting toward the sea, and to avoid looking to the south, where the twin harbors and hundreds of ships would confront him with evidence of human commerce.

When he had rested and eaten and was his usual fast-talking self, she said:

—The Manichees you pray with are crowding our bed.

Does thought exist for the sake of action, or vice versa?

He thought: *If thought exists for the sake of action, I should stop living with her and having sex, because the actions I want ultimately to take are chaste, peaceful, mindful of heaven as my destination.*

If action exists for the sake of thought, I should stop living with her and having sex, because the thoughts I want ultimately to think are pure, rigorous, God-directed.

It was, then, settled. He would leave her. It was time to stop postponing his real life.

But as soon as she returned from the laundry, a glimpse of her long unhurried back or the graceful parenthesis of her neck weakened his ambition and lifted to his lips a compromised prayer:

Lord, give me chastity and abstinence, but not yet.

The boy grew long-limbed and mindful. Augustine said he resembled nothing so much as a piece of string.

—Look who's talking, his concubine joked, poking his visible ribs.

—Cut it out, he said, laughing.

The boy's body grew even more stringlike; his mind took on heft. His father taught him the art of philosophical conversation. Augustine plumed as he and Adeodatus performed for friends, two interlocutors taking on one huge topic after another—immortality of the soul, beauty and tragedy in works of art, the moral life.

—He possesses God who does not have an unclean spirit, said the boy.

Augustine smiled and nodded approvingly, and asked:

—What does this mean, to not have an unclean spirit?

—He does not have an unclean spirit, the boy said, who lives a pure life.

Augustine winked conspiratorially at his audience.

—Ah, he continued, but whom would you call pure, the man who does not sin at all, or the man who refrains only from illicit intercourse?

The boy blushed, turning purple just as his father did when embarrassed. He stared at the ground a moment before speaking.

—How can he be pure, Adeodatus said at last, who refrains only from illicit intercourse but defiles himself in other ways, by other sins? The man who is truly pure applies his mind to God and devotes himself to Him alone.

Augustine looked to his audience proudly.

—Is anyone writing this down? he asked.

The sun threw a red spike into the shoreline. They were naked.

She folded her arms across her chest, smoldering. She stared at him soberly. Her ankles crossed, like a lock closing, forbidding him access.

His face was just above hers. He kissed her upper lip. She turned her head sideways, eyeing him mistrustfully. He stood up. Naked, he looked more wiry and vital than clothed.

Long breakers plunged onto the shore. They did not speak.

He looked at her ear's whorl, which he found mysteriously erotic. Almost against his will he understood suddenly the degree of her sacrifices. She possessed an inner life equal to his own, with its own contradictory urges and fierce debates. He put his hand on the small of her back.

—Can I do anything for you? he said.

—No.

—No?

—No.

In his teens Adeodatus's straight black eyebrows began journeying towards each other, as if overly burdened by Socratic dialogue. The boy's memory and understanding seemed to bloom even more extravagantly in response. When his brow's lacuna closed to within a fingertip's width, Adeodatus outwitted nearly all his father's monastic companions. By the time the eyebrows met in a single stern arch above his thin nose, he could recite all of Virgil's *Eclogues*; none in his father's circle dared engage him on any subject no matter how obscure or difficult; Augustine had already quoted him verbatim in *On the Master*.

Jesus dug a river in the world.

He of the sweet name dug a river.

He dredged it with a basket. The stones He dredged up were like drops of incense.

Among them was my soul freed of lust.

A sparrow fluttered into the morbid room. It darted out the window as quickly as it entered, leaving a bounty of shrill song.

—See? she said.

—What? he said, looking up from his reading.

Is the soul of a centipede in chopped-up portions? Does it have one soul or many tiny souls?

At first his students' questions broke his heart. Eventually he developed affection for the kind dull ones, like Romanian's two sons, Licentius and Trigetius. At least they paid their bills and didn't interrupt his lectures by shouting and whistling at the other pupils. Still, the urge to flee to Rome, where he could expect superior students to line up for classes like his, proved too great.

—I want better students, was all he said to his companion. We're going to Rome.

She heard and understood.

—Is Monica coming? she asked.

—No, he said, surprised, as if the idea hadn't occurred to him.

A sliver of light reached into her. This was his chance escape from his mother. Would he take it? Could he? If she insisted too strongly, he would run back to Monica. But, she knew, he needed to be nudged encouragingly or he would lose momentum.

She looked at the bronze mirror he had given her years ago. Help me, she urged its burnished surfaces, to tread lightly, lightly.

Monica was cooking, the big pots breathing loudly.

—Can she read? she asked civilly.

She gestured for Augustine to start husking corn. He grabbed an ear and tore the green husks in long strips, tossing them into a rattan dish.

—You know she can't, he said impatiently. How many times do we have to have this conversation?

—She's your equal in other ways?

—In other ways my better, he said.

She winced.

—Oh? she said. In what ways is she your better?

—In goodness, in compassion and in patience, he said.

—You know you'll never be able to marry her.

—I know. I know.

—Break it off. Break it off as soon as possible. She's not worthy of you. How long are going to let her drag you down? I'll look after Adeodatus. You know how he takes to me. Don't you see? You could concentrate entirely on your career. When, Aurelius—when will you wake up and take the measure of yourself?

—Mother!

—He did not want to argue. Calming himself, he said:

—Mother, please, my career is a separate issue. The issue here is love. And the only measure of love is to love without measure.

He couldn't believe what had just come out of his mouth. Unexpectedly, it sounded worthy of Cicero, to his ear at least.

—Only a young person could say such a thing, Monica countered. Someday you'll learn this. Are you listening to me?

But he was still savoring his last remark, its justice, its aphoristic balance. Was it possible he was wise in spite of himself? He felt guilty for thinking so. Surely wise men did not congratulate themselves upon making wise utterances. Then, too, he had other things to tell Monica.

—Listen, he said. I need to tell you something. We're sailing to Rome tomorrow. Alypius is there, working as a lawyer, God help him. But he's found me a teaching position which he says will pay more and bring what he calls 'high honors.' And the students are much better than the madmen I teach here. Of course she and Adeodatus are coming with me. I know this is quite a shock.

He exhaled.

The jolt shook her body.

—*What? Tomorrow?* And you're only now telling me? When did this come about?

—I've only just learned. We leave in the morning. Of course you're welcome to come with us.

—I will! I will indeed! Why didn't you tell me you were considering such a move?

—We'll talk on the way to the ship tomorrow. Tonight you can stay at the Saint Cyprian oratory if you like. It's right by the port.

—Oh, Aurelius! Mercy on your soul!

She reached for him, weeping. He stepped back.

—All right then, he said. I'll come by in the morning.

But he did not come by in the morning. By morning his ship had sailed almost to Ostia, having left Carthage the night before. He had lied. He had lied to his tiny, devoted mother, who waited, pacing her room aimlessly, her eyes raw, her jaw sore from clenching, fearing for her son's wasted soul.

A stout wind pushed the merchant ship toward the deep water. Even after the shoreline vanished, gulls appeared out of nowhere to gulp in midair scraps of food. Their cries were piercing, relentless as an infant's. Then night came and the clear, veined moon rose over the sea and the gulls disappeared. Moonlight narrowed the silver distances.

That was last night. Now, approaching Ostia in bright morning, he could not remove from his mind how easily the sea could toss the ship like so much bread in a basket. The ship would pitch and heave. He feared for his life. That the sea was in fact calm and flat (which his concubine pointed out, gently) meant nothing. At any moment, sheer waves might arise and batter them to death, as befits a bald-faced liar like himself. She and Adeodatus, however, deserved better.

Still, even wracked by guilt and sickened by fear, the sea on this, his first voyage, glittered and dazzled, a moving theater of color, utterly indifferent to him. The life in it! In Carthage the sea had at first hypnotized him with its sounds and rich stink only to become part of the daily grind. Now that he was at its mercy, it stung with mystery. Not an aloe leaf but something else entirely, something indescribable.

Their first image of Rome was of a man sewn up in a leather sack and thrown alive into the Tiber River. The man had killed his father. The sack, before being tossed into the brown water by three wreathed thugs, looked as though it contained a playful cat: the paws striking out blindly in one place, then another.

Later in the day they walked along the river to the Theater of Marcellus, where they sat to watch a play by Naevius followed by several boxing matches and a tightrope walker. Before the play began, Augustine gave up his seat to an infirm, elderly man and was ridiculed by the surrounding spectators.

He leaned to his concubine and whispered:

—My God.

—My God, she echoed. What kind of city *is* this?

Rome hammered him, a bright nail, into its merciless teaching cycle. The students were indeed superior but usually skipped on payment days, leaving him with less money than he had in Carthage, but with more students. In a month he hated the Eternal City. His response was to fall ill.

Sweat left his skin cold. His eyes blazed from deep within their sockets. Something raw-toothed tore at his throat and chest.

Was he dying? He thought so.

He groaned feebly at night, coughing, shaking. Finally he couldn't teach any longer and lay in bed throughout the clarifying days, sweating, peeling back the skin of his life and finding underneath a new life wounded but vivid and celibate and devoted to whatever unfathomable presences the words 'God' and 'Christ' pointed to. He now knew. He was now among the knowers. Every created thing was signed by God's Hand, in Christ's blood: the letters legible to whosoever would care to read.

He told no one. In a week he was teaching again, flush with old ardors.

His concubine knew something had happened, something of utmost importance, but he would not say what it was and she could not guess with certainty.

His voice tore the Manichean prayers he loved into fragments, as he himself felt torn. Torn or otherwise, he prayed without ceasing.

                    bound in the body
              mournful earth
                    amnesty of thy
              wind that blows
                          in thy sailing
              wind that blows
                          the sea
                    by thy
                          cry

Did Christ literally rise from the grave?

The Manichees thought not. They believed it was simplistic, even blasphemous, to reduce the mystery and complexity of the resurrection to mundane fact. But Augustine was tiring of Manichean doctrines. Their belief in the Kingdom of Darkness—rivaling, eternally, the Kingdom of Light—no longer satisfied him as an explanation of evil's presence in the world. It suggested a God defenseless against evil, eternally acted upon, without ultimate agency in the battle for the Good and the True. But how could that be, if God was omnipotent?

He was getting a headache. He would ask his concubine to roast mussels in hot stones for dinner. That would cure him.

If God was omnipotent, evil must be an absence of God, an absence of the Good. No created thing could be evil, since God was the creator. Evil, then, could not be counted among the created things. It was a lack, not an entity.

Perhaps he wouldn't be able to wait for the mussels. He might need to snack on some goose eggs beforehand. Had she brought any home from the market?

As for Christ, if He did not rise physically, why did Christians bother to believe anything? Paul himself had said it: "If Christ be not raised, your faith is in vain." Exactly. The resurrection was literally true. The Manichees were wrong. Christ's shroud, a cheesecloth reeking of death, ballooned to earth as it fell from His sleek body. He climbed with the speed of a sparrowhawk to sit at the right hand of the Father.

She had not brought home any goose eggs. He circled their rented rooms, a sparrowhawk himself.

And if Christ arose physically from the grave, what of us? If the resurrection was literally true, which it was, then surely all resurrected bodies—ours as well as Christ's—will enjoy the sweet sleek beauty they attained or should have attained in youth, freed of deformity or corruption.

Yes! he thought, his head pounding, finding at last some dried figs and a cucumber.

One orange sunset, dipping dried dates in honey flavored with thyme, Augustine put his left arm around his concubine's waist and said:

—I'm finished with Rome. Or rather Rome's finished with me. Either way, Symmachus, the Prefect of Milan, has petitioned the Emperor for me. For me! Listen to this: 'Rhetorician to the Imperial Court.' How does that sound?

She smiled, tucked a loose hair into its braid and said:

—You won't have to teach?

—No more teaching. I can scarcely believe it myself. We'll move to Milan at the end of the month. Mother'll join us there.

He licked a dollop of honey from his thumb, and added:

—Milan is where I'll make my fortune.

At once she understood the extent to which her life would be torn asunder.

In no time Monica scoured the landscape of Milanese families and found a wealthy unbetrothed heiress whose father was impressed by Augustine's imperial position. The girl was ten years old, a year and a half short of the legal marriage age. She was light-skinned, small even for her age—a theatrically spoiled child who giggled constantly and showed perfect teeth. After negotiating deftly with the girl's father, Monica signed a contract sealing the deal. Augustine and the girl would wed on her twelfth birthday. He would then receive her considerable dowry.

Adeodatus was fourteen.

Adeodatus's mother, according to the contract, could never again see her son or Augustine.

Right Panel

391 A.D.

A LETTER FROM AURELIUS AUGUSTINE, PRIEST OF HIPPO REGIUS, TO _____, DEVOUT HANDMAID OF GOD, FELLOW SERVANT OF CHRIST AND OF THE MEMBERS OF CHRIST, WARMLY CHERISHED IN CHRIST, WHOM I COMMEND TO THE PROTECTION AND GUIDANCE OF GOD'S MERCY FOR PRESENT AND ETERNAL SALVATION:

I do not know how to begin this letter. This is not because you are unable to read it. I will arrange for my dear Alypius to read it to you.

Our son, Adeodatus, upon whom God bestowed such prodigious powers of intellect and holy gifts of devotion, passed away two years ago today. He was 17 years old. I write to you through a dense fog of grief that has become denser throughout these past two years. That fog is, I know, overcoming you as you read this, making it hard to see, obscuring the most familiar signposts. He is gone. Our Adeodatus is gone. Dear God in heaven!

Why did I wait two years to write you? Well you may ask. When you were so abruptly forced to leave us—when *I* so abruptly forced you to leave us—I promised Our Lord and Savior that I would have no further contact with you, knowing myself to be easily swayed into sinful relations with you. I am breaking that promise. I am breaking it because I should never have made it. Having accepted ordination, I must clear my conscience before helping others to clear theirs.

No. This will not do.

A LETTER FROM AURELIUS AUGUSTINE, PRIEST OF HIPPO
REGIUS, TO _____, DEVOUT HANDMAID OF GOD,
FELLOW SERVANT OF CHRIST AND OF THE MEMBERS
OF CHRIST, WARMLY CHERISHED IN CHRIST, WHOM I
COMMEND TO THE PROTECTION AND GUIDANCE OF
GOD'S MERCY FOR PRESENT AND ETERNAL SALVATION:

Grief is a labyrinth. Grief is full of unexpected cul-de-sacs and passageways
where feeling flares and disappears only to reemerge later in a different cul-
de-sac, a different passageway. Grieving for Adeodatus, unexpectedly,
means grieving for other things as well. I miss you. I miss your warm un-
hurried—

Good Lord, no.

A LETTER FROM AURELIUS AUGUSTINE, PRIEST OF HIPPO
REGIUS, TO _____, DEVOUT HANDMAID OF GOD,
FELLOW SERVANT OF CHRIST AND OF THE MEMBERS
OF CHRIST, WARMLY CHERISHED IN CHRIST, WHOM I
COMMEND TO THE PROTECTION AND GUIDANCE OF
GOD'S MERCY FOR PRESENT AND ETERNAL SALVATION:

This is my third attempt to write a letter to you. What I have to say is literally unthinkable. Our son, Adeodatus—he of the bright mind and graceful reedlike body—has been taken by God to heaven. There he surely cavorts with angels and is accepted into Christ's capacious arms even as we speak.

     Adeodatus died two years ago today.

No. No. No. No.

A LETTER FROM AURELIUS AUGUSTINE, PRIEST OF HIPPO REGIUS, TO _____, DEVOUT HANDMAID OF GOD, FELLOW SERVANT OF CHRIST AND OF THE MEMBERS OF CHRIST, WARMLY CHERISHED IN CHRIST, WHOM I COMMEND TO THE PROTECTION AND GUIDANCE OF GOD'S MERCY FOR PRESENT AND ETERNAL SALVATION:

O God, Founder of the Universe! God, through whom the universe, even with its perverse parts, is perfect! God, to whom dissonance is nothing, since in the end the worst resolves into harmony with the better! God, in whom all things are, yet whom the shame of no creatures in the universe disgraces, nor malice harms, nor error misleads! God, who does not permit any save the pure to know the true! God, Father of Truth, Father of Wisdom, Father of the True and Perfect Life, Father of Blessedness, Father of the Good and the Beautiful, Father of Intelligible Light, Father of our awakening and enlightening, Father of that pledge which warns us to return to Thee!

No. Not now.

A LETTER FROM AURELIUS AUGUSTINE, PRIEST OF HIPPO REGIUS, TO _____, DEVOUT HANDMAID OF GOD, FELLOW SERVANT OF CHRIST AND OF THE MEMBERS OF CHRIST, WARMLY CHERISHED IN CHRIST, WHOM I COMMEND TO THE PROTECTION AND GUIDANCE OF GOD'S MERCY FOR PRESENT AND ETERNAL SALVATION:

I will never send this letter. I realize that now. You who taught me the sweetness of an hour will never learn that our son, Adeodatus, is no longer among the living. Perhaps it is better that way. Perhaps it is better to allow you to imagine (and with such fierce earnestness!) his ascension into the highest academic circles I revolved within in Milan, never mind that we returned to Numidia to pursue mutual lives worthy of Christ.

Or perhaps I am simply a coward, one of the thieves staked beside our Lord and

No. This is helpless.

A LETTER FROM AURELIUS AUGUSTINE, PRIEST OF HIPPO
REGIUS, TO _____, DEVOUT HANDMAID OF GOD,
FELLOW SERVANT OF CHRIST AND OF THE MEMBERS
OF CHRIST, WARMLY CHERISHED IN CHRIST, WHOM I
COMMEND TO THE PROTECTION AND GUIDANCE OF
GOD'S MERCY FOR PRESENT AND ETERNAL SALVATION:

What I'd give not to have
to tell you this   I'd give a level wind
working the bunch grass   sunlight

gliding across Thagaste   the listening
speech of my prayers   the river
of God which is full of water

Adeodatus is dead   Adeodatus is
a mound of rapture and black earth
Our son blessed with holy gifts

of devotion and intellect   17 years
puzzled with us   at the end he cried
for his mother   demanding why I sent you

fragrant ghost   away
For the love of God?   yes
and no   for the love too of severing

our lives   a new vast
world like a wafer on my tongue   O Lord
help me I cannot remember

your face or your face
is a high icon in a dusklit
chapel   Forgive me I will never

tell you this   you will never know
Adeodatus under the grass   you are
as far away as the voice

I want to speak to you with
that voice is like nothing   like nothing
on earth

NOTES

The passages from Virgil are from C. Day Lewis's translation, *The Aeneid of Virgil* (London: Hogarth Press, 1954).

The Manichean hymns are from a collection edited by C. R. C. Allberry, *A Manichaean Psalm-Book (Part II)*, Manichean Manuscripts in the Chester Beatty Collection, Vol. II, 1938.

The information about diviners is from the *Res Gestae* of Ammianus Marcellinus.

The information about tunic styles is from the *Epidicus* of Plautus.

The quotations from Augustine and Plotinus are amalgams of the many available English translations, or at least as many of them as I could find.

This book is dedicated to four beloved, non-Augustinian couples: Susan and Brett, Amy and Joe, Jean and Mike, Jocelyn and Chuck.

Last Poems

IN THE TWENTIETH CENTURY

My brother died in the twentieth century.
I played hopscotch at twilight in the twentieth century.
The dead gave us whiplash in the twentieth century.

I saw the moon shipwrecked in the twentieth century.
I lived in a country of fireflies in the twentieth century.
The dead wanted us all to themselves in the twentieth century.

My brother died in the twentieth century.
I wasted three years on geometry in the twentieth century.
I shed pints of blood in the twentieth century.

The dead exhausted themselves in the twentieth century.
The dead echoed like hammer-strokes in the twentieth century.
The dead drank fistfuls of rainwater in the twentieth century.

I ate sweet apples in the twentieth century.
I ate my peck of dirt in the twentieth century.
I ate my words in the twentieth century.

My father was ten minutes older than the twentieth century.
He shoveled black coal in pitch dark in the twentieth century.
My brother died in the twentieth century.

My mother watched *Gone with the Wind* thirty-two times in the twentieth
    century.
She sold zucchini and rhubarb in the twentieth century.
I wrote ridiculous poems in the twentieth century.

I was incapable of keeping silent in the twentieth century.
My marriage ended in the twentieth century.
My marriage ended in the twentieth century.

I loved Kawasaki in the twentieth century.
I danced like a sumac tree in the twentieth century.
I prayed to the Son of Man in the twentieth century.

I was anesthetized through most of the twentieth century.
I wrote passionate letters in the twentieth century.
I went to a sensitivity workshop and had my umbrella stolen in the
    twentieth century.

The dead jiggled the change in their pockets in the twentieth century.
There was something very obvious in the twentieth century
I could never see or understand.

It was nearly possible to live in the twentieth century.
The dead knocked on the door of my life in the twentieth century.
Who's there? I said in the twentieth century.

NORTH OF THE FUTURE

Did I displace you, Lord, by being here?
Does my body crowd out your body?
Afflict me with Attention Surplus Disorder
so I can see what is in front of my face.

Sunned sparrows dart and mar each other's
minor voices. The imperial River rots
like a stone. Who arranged this barrage
of applause and decay? Ancient of Days, be with me.

Wind panhandles my eyes. Black night licks at my song.
The catalpa tree ponders its canny name.
Lord, move, just this once, yourself out of the way
so I can see the endless spaces you fill without you in them.

Charity, mercy, hope, faith, compassion, love:
a golem made of grief?
I feel his greased limbs circling
in my limbs. And then I don't feel him.

The live world finding a choir is a soul.
The soul is very small: it fits in the hand like a hazelnut.
When I die I will discover
there are people in the world.

ABOUT THE AUTHOR

Tom Andrews grew up in Charleston, West Virginia. He studied at Hope College; at Oberlin College, where he was an intern with *FIELD;* and at the University of Virginia, where he was a Hoyns Fellow. He subsequently taught at Ohio University and at Purdue University. In 1999 he went to Rome, as Poetry Fellow at the American Academy.

His publications include two books of poetry, *The Brother's Country*, a National Poetry Series winner chosen by Charles Wright and published by Persea Books (1990), and *The Hemophiliac's Motorcycle,* winner of the Iowa Poetry Prize and published by the University of Iowa Press (1994). His memoir, *Codeine Diary: True Confessions of a Reckless Hemophiliac* appeared from Harvest Books in 1999. He also edited collections of criticism on two contemporary poets: *On William Stafford: The Worth of Local Things* (University of Michigan Press, 1995), and *The Point Where All Things Meet: Essays on Charles Wright* (Oberlin College Press, 1995).

Tom Andrews fell ill in Athens, Greece, in the summer of 2001 and died in London in July.